Difference and Discrimination in Psychotherapy and Counselling

Other titles in the School of Psychotherapy and Counselling (SPC) Series of Regent's College:

The Heart of Listening
Rosalind Pearmain

Embodied Theories
Emesto Spinelli and Sue Marshall

Wise Therapy
Tim LeBon

Heidegger and the Roots of Existential Therapy
H.W. Cohn

SPC SERIES

Difference and Discrimination in Psychotherapy and Counselling

Sue Marshall

SAGE Publications
London • Thousand Oaks • New Delhi

SAGE Publications Ltd
1 Oliver's Yard
55 City Road
London EC1Y 1SP

SAGE Publications Inc.
2455 Teller Road
Thousand Oaks, California 91320

SAGE Publications India Pvt Ltd
B-42, Panchsheel Enclave
Post Box 4109
New Delhi 100 017

British Library Cataloguing in Publication data

A catalogue record for this book is available
from the British Library

ISBN 1 4129 0117 0
ISBN 1 4129 0118 9 (pbk)

Library of Congress Control Number: 2003115331

Typeset by C&M Digitals (P) Ltd., Chennai, India
Printed in India at Gopsons Papers Ltd, Noida

to Charles
who has always believed in me

to Harry
whose enthusiasm inspires me

and to Alice
who knows what it means to be different

Contents

General Introduction to The SPC Series

I T IS BOTH A GREAT HONOUR and a pleasure to welcome readers to The SPC Series.

The School of Psychotherapy and Counselling at Regent's College (SPC) is one of the largest and most widely respected psychotherapy, counselling and counselling psychology training institutes in the UK. The SPC Series published by Sage marks a major development in the School's mission to initiate and develop novel perspectives centred upon the major topics of debate within the therapeutic professions so that their impact and influence upon the wider social community may be more adequately understood and assessed.

A brief overview of SPC

Although its origins lie in an innovative study programme developed by Antioch University, USA, in 1977, SPC has been in existence in its current form since 1990. SPC's MA in Psychotherapy and Counselling Programme obtained British validation with City University in 1991. More recently, the MA in Existential Counselling Psychology obtained accreditation from the British Psychological Society. SPC was also the first UK institute to develop a research-based MPhil/PhD Programme in Psychotherapy and Counselling, and this has been validated by City University since 1992. Largely on the impetus of its first Dean, Emmy van Deurzen, SPC became a full training and accrediting member of the United Kingdom Council for Psychotherapy (UKCP) and countinues to maintain a strong and active presence in that organization through its Professional Members, many of whom also hold professional affiliations with the British Psychological Society (BPS), the British Association of Counselling and Psychotherapy (BACP), the Society for Existential Analysis (SEA) and the European Society for Communicative Psychotherapy (ESCP).

SPC's other programmes include: a Foundation Certificate in Psychotherapy and Counselling, Advanced Professional Diploma Programmes in Existential Psychotherapy and Integrative Psychotherapy, and a series of intensive Continuing Professional Development and related adjunct courses such as its innovative Legal and Family Mediation Programmes.

With the personal support of the President of Regent's College, Mrs Gillian Payne, SPC has recently established the Psychotherapy and Counselling Consultation Centre housed on the college campus which provides individual and group therapy for both private individuals and organizations.

As a unique centre for learning and professional training, SPC has consistently emphasized the comparative study of psychotherapeutic theories and techniques while paying careful and accurate attention to the philosophical assumptions underlying the theories being considered and the philosophical coherence of those theories to their practice-based standards and professional applications within a diversity of private and public settings. In particular, SPC fosters the development of faculty, and graduates who think independently are theoretically well informed and able skilfully and ethically to apply the methods of psychotherapy and counselling in practice, in the belief that knowledge advances through criticism and debate, rather than uncritical adherence to received wisdom.

The integrative attitude of SPC

The underlying ethos upon which the whole of SPC's educational and training programme rests is its *integrative attitude*, which can be summarized as follows.

There exists a multitude of perspectives in current psychotherapeutic thought and practice, each of which expresses a patricular philosophical viewpoint on an aspect of being human. No one single perspective or set of underlying values and assumptions is universally shared.

Given that a singular, or shared, view does not exist, SPC seeks to enable a learning environment which allows competing and diverse models to be considered both conceptually and experientially so that their areas of interface and divergence can be exposed, considered and clarified. This aim espouses the value of holding the tension between contrasting and often contradictory ideas, of 'playing with' their experiential possibilities and of allowing a paradoxical security which can 'live with' and at times even thrive in the absence of final and fixed truths.

SPC defines this aim as 'the integrative attitude' and has designed all of its courses so that its presence will challenge and stimulate all aspects of our students' and trainees' learning experience. SPC believes that this deliberate engagement with difference should be reflected in the manner in which the faculty relate to students, clients and colleagues at all levels. In such a way this attitude may be seen as the lived expression of the foundational ethos of SPC.

The SPC Series

The SPC Series seeks to provide readers with wide-ranging, accessible and pertinent texts intended to challenge, inspire and influence debate in a variety of issues and areas central to therapeutic enquiry. The Series reflects SPC's internationally acknowledged ability to address key topics from an informed, critical and non-doctrinal perspective.

The continuing expansion of texts within the SPC Series expresses what is hoped will be a long and fruitful relationship between SPC and Sage. More than that, there exists the hope that the series will become identified by professionals and public alike as an invaluable contribution to the advancement of psychotherapy and counselling as vigorously self-critical, socially minded and humane professions.

PROFESSOR ERNESTO SPINELLI
Series Editor

Acknowledgements

I F I WERE TO TRACE BACK THE thoughts, ideas, events and conversations that have culminated in the writing of this book, I would have to credit the original impetus of the project to the inspirational teaching of June Roberts, whose seminar on social issues I took one spring in the early 1990s. June died in 2000, sadly, but I would like to think that some of her passion, energy and her attitude of challenging orthodoxy live on in the pages that follow.

I have gained much in my professional career from the many students I have taught. Their input and ideas are also represented in this book – I am grateful both to them and for the richness of experience that teaching others always provides.

I would like to thank the many people who have helped me in a number of ways throughout the writing of this book. My first acknowledgement has to go to Ernesto Spinelli, whose encouragement and help inspired me to think about making a beginning. Many friends and colleagues have provided support along the way. In particular I would like to thank Sarah-Gay Fletcher, Marilyn Foster, Sue Kork, Michael Montier, Kelly Noel-Smith, Boo Orman, Beryl Semple and Frances Wilks – their friendship, professional input and belief in me have been invaluable. Very special thanks must go to Tato Bromley, whose tireless work in helping with research and typing has made the whole project possible within the deadlines set.

Finally, I would like to thank my family for their consistent and tireless interest, support and encouragement throughout this project.

Introduction

IN MY OWN EXPERIENCE AS A therapist, supervisor and trainer I have frequently been struck by the dangers of ignoring or minimizing social reality. The majority of the trainees, students, supervisees and colleagues I have encountered over the years have, like myself, come from backgrounds which would not necessarily expose them to the kinds of attitudes, prejudices and adverse discrimination which, unfortunately, still pervade our society. I have come across lamentable ignorance, which is excusable, and occasionally a blinkered unwillingness to challenge this ignorance, which is not. On this count, what I am hoping to provide in this book is some information that will remove the blinkers and fill in some of the gaps. The BACP *Ethical Framework for Good Practice in Counselling and Psychotherapy* states that 'the practitioner is responsible for learning about and taking account of the different protocols, conventions and customs that can pertain to different working contexts and cultures' (BACP, 2002: 9), which is a considerable improvement on their previous code of ethics which merely mentioned 'sensitivity to cultural context'. We do need more than sensitivity – we need understanding and we cannot understand without information and learning.

As counsellors and therapists, as well as increasing our knowledge about what goes on out there in society, we need to understand what is going on inside ourselves – what is commonly referred to in the trade as 'self-awareness'. I have always understood this to mean owning up to all the nasty bits – not necessarily to anyone else, though under the right circumstances that can be very therapeutic – but primarily to one's self. I believe we all hold views which have the potential to be discriminatory, prejudiced or exclusionary; I believe we all have difficulty, in some degree, with people who are in some significant way different from ourselves. On this count what I am hoping this text might do, for readers who may not have explored fully this part of their being, is to challenge them to do so. In the BACP *Ethical Framework* we find the statement, 'Practitioners should not allow their professional relationships with clients to be prejudiced by any personal views they may hold about lifestyle, gender, age, disability, race, sexual orientation, beliefs or culture' (BACP, 2002: 7). The implication of this is that practitioners may well hold views on such matters which *could* prejudice their professional relationships. What is missing (although perhaps implicit) in this statement is the recognition of the need for practitioners to be aware of what those views are. The previous BAC *Code of Ethics* did not pull any punches; it stated categorically that 'counsellors have a responsibility to consider and address their own prejudices and stereotyping attitudes and behaviour' (BAC, 1998: B.2.4). This is what I think we need more of – too many of us, therapists, counsellors, supervisors, trainers, do not sufficiently consider and address such attitudes and behaviour in ourselves.

In the course of my research for this book I conducted an informal survey of counselling services and training courses throughout the UK. It was by no means comprehensive, but served as a useful straw poll of some of the characteristics of those engaged in the enterprises of counselling and psychotherapy. In the questionnaire sent out I posed questions first about the gender and racial or ethnic origin of counsellors, clients, training staff and students. Most organizations who returned the questionnaire were willing to supply this information. I also asked questions about the psychiatric history of the same group. This yielded less information. Part of the questionnaire was devoted to the content of training courses and the extent to which topics such as race, gender, sexual orientation and mental illness are covered, if at all. The information that I gleaned from this survey forms the basis for many of the assertions in the first chapter, and elsewhere in the book.

The first chapter consists of an overview of some of the themes that occur and recur in connection with all the subjects examined in this text: identity, our response to difference, the nature of prejudice, and the debates around nature and nurture as well as around sameness and equality. The chapters that follow are all devoted to a particular topic – an element of being which has the potential to attract adverse discrimination. Within these chapters I have begun with a historical overview of each particular subject, and then attempted to analyse the themes and theories that surround it. There follows an examination and discussion of the relationship between the topic and the psychotherapeutic enterprise. In Chapter 5, on mental illness, there is a further section devoted to some of the intersections between all the subjects covered in the book. My discussions centre principally on the western world – Europe, the USA and, in particular, the UK.

The scope of this book is necessarily limited. In order to do justice to the topics I wanted to cover, I had to restrict the number of topics that could be included. Apart from the four subjects I have examined – race and culture, gender, sexuality and mental illness – there are many others that are equally significant within the context of discrimination and difference. Disability, class, age and religion spring immediately to mind, and there are many more. I would like to emphasize that I have not excluded such topics on the grounds of seeing them as less worthy of study, but on the grounds of pragmatism and lack of space. I was faced with some invidious and difficult choices. There is much scope for further fruitful work in this field to examine other elements of experience where issues of difference and discrimination play a significant role.

1 | Discrimination, Difference and Identity

EACH INDIVIDUAL PERSON IS unique. Our uniqueness defines us and separates us. It may also be the source of our delight in each other and enrich our personal relationships. Over and above our uniqueness we also share characteristics with other people – some characteristics with almost everybody else, others with only a few. Common features, like unique qualities, can also form the basis of connections and relationships between people and groups. So, in varying degrees, we are like and unlike other people we encounter. Despite the fact that most people are able to tolerate, even celebrate and enjoy, the unique differences of others with whom they come into contact, in general we are most comfortable in the company of those with whom we share common features. Such features may be social class, educational background, taste in music, religious beliefs, professional interests and a whole host of other possible factors. The more we have 'in common' with another person, the more likely we are to feel an affinity with them. Differences, too, may be a source of interest, but they are potentially more challenging and divisive. There is a level of comfort in being able to identify with elements of another person's being or experience.

History and observation demonstrate that our response to differentness is not universally one of acceptance. Neither is it universally one of condemnation and rejection. I would maintain, however, that it is more often a response which veers away from inclusion and tends towards withdrawal. Such withdrawal can take many forms – some relatively benign, others with a greater capacity for causing offence or damage. Prejudice and adverse discrimination exist in all social groups. The fact that there are laws against discrimination of various kinds in every western country attests to its existence. You do not need to outlaw something unless it has proved to be problematic. Such laws have helped by punishing offenders – people who have been shown to be actively practising racism or sexism or some other form of discrimination – and, presumably, by acting as deterrents. The deterrent effect would be to discourage people from engaging in overt expressions of prejudices, but would do nothing to remove the underlying beliefs, thoughts and feelings which motivate such expressions. It would be convenient to assume that the phenomena of prejudice and adverse discrimination manifest themselves in a small and reprehensible group within society and that most of us are in the clear – unbiased and prejudice-free. I do not believe this to be the case. Fortunately, it is only a small minority who choose to engage in the most extreme forms of discriminatory behaviour – violence or even murder on the basis of a person's skin colour, religion or sexual orientation. But that does not exonerate the rest of us from harbouring prejudices. We all have preferences and we discriminate, in the sense of making choices based on our values and tastes, in all areas of our lives. Many of these choices and preferences are in response to the perceived similarities and differences of others. And it is in these responses, I believe, that the potential for prejudice is present in all of us.

The presence of our own prejudices or biases is something we prefer not to acknowledge or examine, precisely because it conflicts with that aspect of our chosen identity by which we would like to see ourselves as non-judgemental, fair-minded, accepting of all humankind. How, then, do we address it? Only by scrupulously honest and searching self-examination. This can be achieved on our own, in dialogue with others, maybe in therapy or with close friends. But, like all dimensions of self-discovery, it cannot be forced upon us by others. You can take a horse to water, or a client to therapy, but … as the saying goes. I suspect that many students of counselling or psychotherapy sit through their mandatory hours of therapy while in training without really looking too closely at some of those parts of their inner life that they are least happy about. In writing this book I am hoping, possibly vainly, to provoke in the reader the impulse to look within and own some of those uncomfortable, possibly deeply hidden, prejudices and dislikes.

There are many facts and much information within these pages. This is intentional. By remaining ignorant it is easier to hold on to the belief that we live in a just and equitable society. Once we have learnt that things are not quite how we would like them to be, it becomes harder to deceive ourselves and also, I hope, harder to maintain the pretence that we are not part of the system. Society is made of people – you and me and him and her. If the society we have created is imperfect, unjust, pernicious or oppressive it is because we have made it so, or allowed it to be so made.

In any interview process for counselling training courses, one of the things that causes me the greatest disquiet is an attitude of 'them' and 'us'; the candidate who feels that he/ she would like to 'help' those poor afflicted souls who are troubled and need some 'direction' in their lives. I believe you are only of any benefit as a counsellor or therapist if you see clients' issues in terms of being part of the human predicaments and problems which affect us all, yourself included. By the same token, the person who retreats behind the clichés of 'Some of my best friends are black/ gay' or 'I don't have a problem with the disabled/lesbians' is taking the 'them' and 'us' stance, as well as laying claim to a position of total impartiality which I suspect conceals an unwillingness to own the inner prejudices we all possess. I am not trying to suggest that there is not a distinction between overt racist violence and the moral position of most members of society. It is, however, too easy to disown our own prejudices by focusing on the more extreme manifestations of adverse discrimination. We are, by definition, part of society and the inequalities within its structure and institutions are but a reflection of the biases and values of each individual member of which society is constituted.

One of the recurring themes in this book is identity. Our individual identity is made up of a vast number of components which intersect with and interact upon one another; there is an artificiality about attempting to tease them apart, to isolate them and analyse them separately. And yet that is what I have attempted to do in order to examine the nature of the responses that are evoked by individual elements of differentness. It is important to bear in mind that each person is many other things as well as that element of his/her identity that has the potential to provoke a response of prejudice or discrimination. This has been highlighted by the lobby who urge use of the term 'gay men' instead of the term 'gays'. Using the word 'gay' as a noun implies the identification of a group of people by their sexual preference, as though that and that alone defined them as people. Society, however, still regularly refers to 'gays', 'lesbians', 'the disabled', 'the mentally ill' – a tendency which fosters the false assumption of homogeneity in such groups as well as having the effect of defining people by a single element of who they are. Both of these processes – the assumption of homogeneity and the defining of people by one aspect of their being – are central to the process of adverse discrimination.

The subjects I have chosen to examine are all ones which attract the highest levels of social interest and concern – and of discrimination and prejudice. For those of us, like myself, who are in the majority group for most elements of social identity – white, heterosexual, able-bodied, free of a psychiatric diagnosis, middle-class, educated – it is hard to imagine the experience of those who are not. It is all too easy to deny the extent to which elements of being such as skin colour or sexual orientation (among many) incite responses from others that are experienced as alienating, exclusionary, rejecting or demeaning. In her book *Mixed Feelings*, Yasmin Alibhai-Brown writes, 'however mixed-race couples and mixed-race children choose to live their lives, they cannot shake off historical baggage or isolate themselves from the assumptions and bigotries of the outside world' (Alibhai-Brown, 2001: 14). You could substitute many words for the phrase 'mixed-race couples and mixed-race children' in that passage: 'gay men and lesbian women', 'black and coloured people', 'disabled people', 'people with a mental illness'. Being in a non-normative minority group means you are rarely able to forget about that element of who you are which sets you apart from the majority, and which has the potential to provoke responses in others that include feelings of fear, dislike, repulsion, prejudice or hatred.

In recent years there has been a heightened awareness of the implications of social prejudice and discrimination. Many minority groups have formed organizations to protest against inequitable treatment and lobby for political and social reform. A commonplace response to such movements goes something like this: 'I can't understand why such an issue is made of being homosexual/black [or whatever the focus is]. I never make an issue of being heterosexual/white – it's just part of who I am!' What such a viewpoint fails to realize is that the ability to take for granted any crucial element of identity is a luxury only afforded those who belong to the dominant majority group. Outside that, the attitude of the dominant group means that however much you might want to take being black, or gay, or disabled for granted, you are not allowed to because you are constantly reminded, on a daily basis, that most people around you have difficulty, in some way, with that part of who you are – and that many never see beyond it to the rest of the person.

The concept of identity raises questions such as: Who am I? Where do I belong? How do I fit in to this or that group of people? One of the basic human quests is that of trying to make sense of the world around us. We are constantly searching for meaning in the experiences we encounter. We also seek to organize our world into structure and routine in order to make ourselves feel more comfortable. Disruption of routine or an experience which shakes our sense of structure can induce anxiety, a sense of being undermined, lost and alone. One of the elements which contribute to our sense of structure and meaning is that of identity. Much has been written on the development of human identity: how and at what stage it develops, the critical elements that contribute to or detract from its secure formation, and so on. In western psychology it is generally accepted that knowing who you are, in the sense of where you come from and how you fit into a given social group or family, is crucial for psychological health. Research in the field of adoption would seem to support this notion (Verrier, 1993). But as well as wanting to know who you are in the sense of where you came from genealogically, the question 'Who am I?' seems to refer to something internal and personal – something unique to you alone. However, the two seem to be intimately linked.

To begin with 'external' identity: if you ask someone to list the elements by which they define their identity it is likely they will enumerate a variety of things – gender, age, marital status, nationality, occupation, perhaps religion, sexual orientation or social class. Many of these elements exist in polarities – man/woman, straight/gay, black/white and so on. They also indicate not only individual identity but membership of a group. I am a woman, but my understanding of that concept can only make sense in the context of recognizing that there are other beings whose characteristics (those that indicate femaleness) I share. Furthermore, the concept of femaleness has no meaning in isolation. It only carries meaning in contrast with another group of beings who share characteristics that indicate maleness. Thus a central part of the formation of our individual identity consists of identifying those groups to which we belong and those to which we do not belong. In other words, we confirm who we are by comparison with others – by differentiating elements of sameness and elements of difference. This appears to be a process that goes on all our lives and is a vital part of the development of an inner sense of ourselves as a unique and valuable individual.

The comparisons we make encompass more than external characteristics. They extend to tastes and preferences, aptitudes and abilities, emotional and psychological elements – the whole complex web of personality and being that constitutes who we are. External identity, however, as the first element by which we perceive another person, has a particular impact. All too often we draw inferences about a person's internal being from our perception of their external appearance or their way of presenting themselves. It would seem, therefore, that we form an internal sense of identity as a direct result of observations we make of other people and of ourselves in relation to them. As I said at the outset, we are all unique, but that uniqueness can only emerge in the context of elements of sameness and difference – in relation to the world around us and our response to it.

Differentiation and comparison of self with other are part of human interactions from the earliest moments of life. The early stages of infancy include the process of individual differentiation of the baby from the mother. Response to difference, too, is observable very early – small children are fearful of someone unfamiliar and schoolchildren are quick to tease anyone who looks different: the redhead, the fat child, the boy with glasses. There seems to be a need to feel that we are the same as others, the need to identify with other people in a group. Is this perhaps part of a need to reinforce our own sense of identity? It seems as though we need to see ourselves mirrored in another person as a way of validating who we are – almost an affirmation of our existence. It is significant that a baby's first interactions with his/her mother take the form of a mirroring process – an endless reflection back and forth of gestures, movements and facial expressions. As teenagers most of us go through a phase where similarity to our peer group is vitally important. Adolescents go to extraordinary lengths to adopt the same manner of dress, hairstyle, body shape, tastes and vocabulary as those around them. It would seem to be an essential part of the process of establishing our own unique identity to begin with a sense of group identity – to first be the same as everyone else. Most people develop beyond this phase as part of the process of gaining maturity. They become able to claim their own uniqueness, which allows them to feel comfortable about being different from others in some ways, and also to feel relatively at ease in the presence of others whom they perceive as different.

However, I believe we never completely lose that deep need to be among those who are like us and who therefore reinforce our security in who we are. Most people's closest friendships are with those who would fall into that group. This is not to say that people do not often form deep and lasting friendships and relationships with someone who is, in some sense, 'other' – but in such situations we will, if possible, maintain a pool of friends whose similarities to ourselves provide that sense of validation which we seem to need. Being with people whom we perceive to be the same or similar has the effect of affirming our own identity – of reinforcing our perhaps fragile sense that who and what we are is basically acceptable. By the same token, being in the presence of those who in some significant way we perceive to be different, can undermine that sense of basic acceptability. For this reason I believe we all have difficulty, to varying degrees, in fully accepting the presence in our midst of someone who is noticeably different in some way – their existence has the power, fundamentally, to threaten our own. I am not mirrored in this person, so do I exist at all?

Our discomfort with difference thus has the potential to undermine our own sense of identity. One way of decreasing the tension inherent in this situation is to make the different person into the 'Other' – to retreat psychologically into group identity and stigmatize those outside the group. Reinforcing our own sense of belonging in a group is obtained by the exclusion of others. My sense of being part of the 'in' group is strengthened by identifying who is in the 'out' group. Indeed, there is no 'in' group without an 'out' group, just as the concept of 'woman' makes no sense without the existence of men. This process of exclusion by comparison is one that has occurred throughout history to all groups identified as outside the social mainstream for whatever reason. That the establishment of group identity is psychologically reassuring is further demonstrated by the social movements which arose in the 1960s. Identity politics created the notion of claiming one's identity as a member of an oppressed or marginalized group as a political point of departure. Such politics involve the celebration of a group's uniqueness as well as protest against its particular oppression. Thus the source of your exclusion from the mainstream – your difference and 'outcast' status – becomes your passport to inclusion in a new group. On a different level the proliferation and success of self-help groups demonstrates the same process at work.

It is no longer socially sanctioned to engage in openly hostile or discriminatory behaviour towards people whose appearance, life-style or beliefs are different from our own – which is not to say that such behaviour does not occur.

Most people have no difficulty with an intellectual acceptance of someone with a different skin colour, gender, religion or sexual preference from their own. But is there something deeper than such an intellectual stance – some deep aversion to difference within us all? In other words, is adverse discrimination a human universal? It would certainly seem to be the case that we all need to feel we belong, and we all struggle with acceptance of difference in others. As we have seen, these two are inextricably linked – our identities are forged by the marking of difference. Identity depends on difference, and therefore on discrimination.

The subject of differences between people immediately raises questions about the source of such differences and about the relative merits of the various elements of discrepancy. The nature/nurture debate is another theme which runs through all the topics examined in this book. Are differences innate or are they the result of environmental influences? This seems to be intimately connected to another question: does equality of treatment have to rest on notions of sameness? As we shall see, the confusion between these two questions has led to much (unnecessary) debate and muddled thinking.

Historically, biological theories have been invoked to justify the worst excesses of adverse discrimination. Black people and Jews have been seen as biologically different, defective and inferior; women have been viewed as by nature less intelligent, capable and rational than men; homosexuals have been characterized as inherently mentally ill or suffering from warped or incomplete development. Such justifications have led to a variety of inequitable and inhumane forms of treatment, ranging from social exclusion and oppression to eugenics. By viewing the different 'other' as an inferior form of human life, or even as less than human, we can argue for the differential treatment of groups of people based on assumed immutable differences. We can even argue that differential treatment is for their own good. Their lack of civilization, or intelligence, or psychological development, rooted as it is in their genes or their biology represents an inequality which demands a different response. Clearly this is an argument that can have the effect of making us more comfortable about social inequity. In its extreme forms, biological determinism has been used as the basis for racist and sexist ideologies which today incite moral repugnance. As we have reacted against such extreme forms of discriminatory behaviour, so too have we reacted against their underlying ideologies. In order to argue for equal treatment for different social groups, it has seemed vital to argue for equal potential – the concept of 'the blank slate' (Pinker, 2002), which asserts that everyone starts life with the same possibilities and there are no innate biological differences. This has led to the doctrine of social constructionism or social determinism – the view that any perceived differences between individuals or groups of individuals are the product of environment, upbringing, diet, education and so forth, and nothing to do with biology or genetic inheritance. But this was, in effect, throwing the baby out with the bathwater. Acknowledging innate biological differences does not have to involve an evaluation of their respective worth.

Difference does not have to mean better or worse, but it is very often taken to mean so. If we assume that a judgement of something as different has to involve an evaluation of better or worse, then to achieve equality we have to argue for sameness. When sameness is manifestly not apparent, the differences are explained by lack of opportunity, environmental factors, and so on – the social constructionist stance. This can be seen within the arguments surrounding the relative positions of men and women within our society. To say that men and women have innate differences (apart from their obvious physical ones) sets up echoes of centuries of arguments which claimed that the biology of women made them intellectually, psychologically and emotionally inferior to men. Difference was used as a synonym for inferiority. To counter that, it is necessary to argue that women are the *same* as men – intellectually, psychologically and emotionally – and therefore their equals. Equality of biological endowment demands equality of treatment. If or when men and women demonstrate differences in aptitude or inclination in certain areas of activity, such differences can only be explained by indoctrination or discrimination – not by any innate preferences or predispositions. The waters are muddied by the fact that indoctrination and discrimination still take place, but absurd positions have been taken in the attempt to disprove the existence of innate differences between the genders.

There is, however, an alternative, which is to say that different means just that – different. Equally valid, not better or worse. This notion is now in the social and political domain and is central to the concept of multiculturalism. The phrases 'valuing difference' and 'celebrating difference' appear regularly in the media and in sociological literature. But it appears to be a concept with which we have considerable difficulty – perhaps for all the reasons I suggested concerning our need for establishing and maintaining our identity. Making comparisons between ourselves and others seems to be part of basic human psychology, and comparison automatically takes us into the realm of differences and, seemingly, comparative worth. It also takes us away from the process of looking for areas of similarity or common ground. As Steven Pinker argues (2002: xi), the acknowledgement of human nature, of innate human characteristics, has the potential to 'expose the psychological unity of our species beneath the superficial differences of physical appearance and parochial culture'. Our fear of admitting that there are innate differences between individuals or groups of individuals stems from the historical use of biological theories to justify the worst manifestations of prejudice and discrimination. I believe it also stems from the fear of being fixed or determined by such innate properties. However, even a committed Darwinian like Richard Dawkins concedes that humans possess a quality unique in the animal kingdom – the power to make choices that override our genes (Dawkins, 1976: 200). I return to Steven Pinker, who states forcibly:

> The case against bigotry is not a factual claim that humans are biologically indistinguishable. It is a moral stance that condemns judging individuals according to the average traits of certain groups to which the individual belongs. (Pinker, 2002: 145)

What emerges then is the vital need to see differences as elements that should be acknowledged and taken into account in all human relationships, without either evaluating them or allowing them to blind us to the presence of similarities. Some differences may be innate, some may be culturally or socially determined. Their origin may well be of intellectual or academic interest but should not influence our response to them. It seems clear, however, that the response of discomfort with or fear of difference *is* a universal human tendency. Nevertheless we possess, as with our genes, the power to confront and reverse that tendency. It is that tendency, within ourselves, with which we should be battling, not the 'Other' as personified by the outcast in the form of the black or disabled person, or the gay or lesbian men and women we encounter.

What are the implications of our understanding of the nature of prejudice, discrimination and response to difference for the enterprises of counselling and psychotherapy? If adverse discrimination and social prejudice lead to psychological distress, which they clearly do, and if counselling and psychotherapy are in the business of alleviating psychological distress, which they claim to be, one would expect to find a high concentration of psychotherapeutic services devoted to minority groups, or at the very least a statistical representation of such groups within the clients of counselling and psychotherapy proportional to their presence within society at large. Sadly, neither is the case. There are indeed services devoted to counselling with minority cultural or racial groups, and with lesbian women and gay men, but such facilities are few and tend to be concentrated geographically in large cities, in particular in London. Within the field of counselling and psychotherapy as a whole clients from minority groups of any kind are significantly under-represented.

Why should this be so? I think the answer is very simple. Given that we appear to have a natural tendency to gravitate towards people with whom we have shared characteristics, and a need to feel part of a group, is it not possible or even likely that in our work as well as our social lives this should also apply? If we work as counsellors or therapists, the implications are that we would therefore feel more comfortable with, accept as clients, work more productively with, people with whom we have a natural affinity based on such criteria as race, social group, sexual orientation, gender, and so forth. As the vast majority of counsellors, therapists and trainers in this field are white, educated, heterosexual women, this would appear to place potential clients or trainee counsellors who fall into categories other than those in a disadvantageous position. In an ideal world all counsellors, therapists and trainers will have, in their own training, addressed their internal prejudices in such a way that would remove the possibility of the kind of bias I am suggesting. But the world is far from ideal and I fear this is very often not the case. It is no surprise, therefore, to discover that the majority of clients (and trainee counsellors and therapists) are also white, middle-class heterosexual women. This would be acceptable, though regrettable, if the enterprises of counselling and psychotherapy acknowledged that they existed primarily to provide a service to a particular, narrow sector of society. This, however, is not the case. These enterprises pride themselves on being non-judgemental, non-discriminatory and inclusive. The very basis of much of their theory rests on such notions.

Many would-be counsellors come into training with an assumption that they must somehow demonstrate their ability to be non-judgemental. I suspect that they therefore seek to hide (from themselves and others) any prejudices they may have, in the fear that disclosure of such would disqualify them from the training they are undergoing or hoping to undergo. The task of all counsellors and therapists and all training courses has to be to challenge such notions. We need to be able to admit to the biases and prejudices that are an inevitable part of our make-up in order to have any hope of relating to our clients in a way which allows them to face their inner prejudices, or indeed explore with us the ways in which they are different from us or others and the impact of being on the receiving end of adverse discrimination. Many training courses now include factors such as gender, sexual orientation, race and culture, and working with difference within their curriculum. Many still do not. All too often the focus of the teaching in these subjects is on underlying internal psychological mechanisms; little attention is paid to the impact of prejudice and social discrimination in the external world. Little attention, too, is given to the trainees' own prejudices. Most training courses have the unfortunate effect of reinforcing dominant culture stereotyping. This is precisely because the theory and practice they teach are based on the values and norms of the dominant group in society – white, middle-class, educated and heterosexual.

It would appear, therefore, that the enterprises of counselling and psychotherapy run a severe risk of being normative, of becoming not only channels through which the values and life-style norms of the majority group are reinforced but also instruments of maintaining the status quo by helping people 'adjust' to the inequalities within society.

Some people have even suggested a more sinister agenda in that such an activity has the effect of defusing energy that might otherwise be directed towards social activism. Such an argument would depict counselling and therapy as active agents of social control (Hillman and Ventura, 1992). I would not go as far as that, but I think there is a worrying tendency to skate over issues of difference and, in particular, the psychological impact of social discrimination. If counselling and psychotherapy have any hope of being truly inclusive then each individual practitioner has to be able to own his or her individual prejudices. Over and above that, in working with clients from minority groups the focus has to be on more than intra-psychic processes. The problems of those who are the recipients of discrimination are not best explained or understood by mechanisms such as oedipal complexes, denial, splitting and so forth. These problems have to be seen in an inter-relational context (Spinelli, 2001) and a social context (Williams, 1999). The challenges that arise in working with differences are particularly severe because they force (or should force) therapists to own and work through those parts of themselves which are least socially acceptable – and indeed which run counter to many of the underlying assumptions within counselling and therapy training – their own prejudices, fears and internal biases. My hope is that we are up to the challenge.

2 | Race and Culture

THE SUBJECT OF RACE AND CULTURE, and our response to it, abounds with expressions and terms which are often confusing in their usage. Is there such a thing as 'race' in the sense of a means by which to distinguish, with any precision, between groups of people? What is the connection between race and culture? Sometimes the two seem to coincide quite precisely – the culture of a particular group corresponds with their distinctiveness as a race, or ethnic group. In other instances the overlap is less exact, the boundaries are blurred; two 'racial groups' appear to share a similar culture, or one 'racial group' displays evidence of different cultural traditions.

The focus of this chapter is on the ways in which the response to a person's race or culture (or both) is one which includes adverse discrimination – prejudice against that person because of this element of difference and consequentially differential treatment. There are many terms which have been used to describe this response: racism, nationalism, xenophobia, tribalism, ethnocentrism, group prejudice, or simply a sense of family or kinship. Our use of language can make something sound either relatively benign or potentially evil and sinister. It is important, therefore, to begin by attempting to define some terms.

When we talk about a person's race we are generally making distinctions based on appearance and physical characteristics. Underlying this are beliefs (correct or otherwise) about the involuntary effects of genetic inheritance. When we talk about culture or ethnicity we are referring to the customs, social practices (and perhaps religion) that a person chooses to follow or engage in. Race, therefore, refers to those characteristics over which we have no choice – they are a given, and may or may not include elements endowed by inheritance which are specific to a particular group. It is this distinction that informs the definition of 'racism' as used by modern historians. When differences are regarded as innate and unchangeable *and* are used as a justification for persecution or discriminatory treatment, based on distinctions of superiority and inferiority attributed to those supposed innate differences, then we have racism. If there is the possibility for the Other to change, for example by religious conversion or cultural assimilation, what is in operation is bigotry, prejudice or xenophobia, but not racism (MacMaster, 2001; Fredrickson, 2002). That is not to say that prejudice and discrimination based on religion or culture are any less painful (or dangerous) for those who are its recipients. Indeed Fredrickson (2002: 7) concedes that 'culturalism' can work in the same way as racism, where culture is viewed as essentialist and unchangeable and social groups (for example, modern immigrants to England and France) are for that reason assumed to be unable to assimilate.

Racism, by this definition therefore, is both an ideology and a form of behaviour. It is based on theories which posit unbridgeable differences between ethnic groups, and then uses those distinctions to justify social exclusion, segregation, persecution or genocide. Central to the process of racism is the identification of differences, usually the most visible, which then become symbolic markers for racial classification and the attribution of essential forms of moral, mental and cultural inferiority. The predominant forms of western racism are white supremacy and anti-Semitism. They are also the forms that have been manifested in the most extreme manner in recent history. The word racism entered the European language in the 1930s 'to identify the doctrine that race determines culture, the underlying concept being that of race as type' (Banton, 1997: 40). The connection between race and culture is, by this definition, seen as central, with the suggestion that culture, too, is in some way fixed. Banton identifies the 1960s as the time when 'racism' took on new meanings; it came to refer to beliefs and attitudes used to subordinate, control or exploit groups of people defined in racial terms, and in more general terms to refer to almost anything connected with racial discrimination, prejudice and inequality. He makes the distinction between the bias which causes people to interpret events, and to judge other people, in the light of their own society's values – a phenomenon he calls 'ethnocentricism' – and prejudice, which he defines as a 'rigid and hostile attitude towards members of particular groups that often has sources in the psychology of the person in question' (Banton, 1997: 34). In Banton's view ethnocentricism, unlike prejudice, is an essentially benign phenomenon. Other writers have made different distinctions. Fredrickson describes ethnocentricism, which he calls 'a virtually universal phenomenon in group contacts' as 'the tendency to discriminate against the stranger, the alien, the physically different' (Fredrickson, 1988). In common language usage this latter definition is what most people would describe as racism, in other words the prejudice and the behaviour without the underlying ideology. Indeed, an even narrower usage of the word 'racism' would confine it to discrimination on the grounds of physical appearance, specifically skin colour. And yet anti-Semitism is undeniably a form of racism. It could be argued that Jews have distinctive physical characteristics, but probably no more than, say, Italians or Norwegians. Such physical characteristics are by no means universal or as immediately apparent as skin colour. The factors in anti-Semitism relate more to culture or religion or life-style, as presumed identifiers of a racial group.

While acknowledging the pertinence of historians' semantic distinctions, and the powerful argument that what made historical events such as the Holocaust, black slavery in the USA, and apartheid in South Africa distinctive, was the presence of an ideology which lent particular and pernicious weight to these events and situations, I would argue that the word 'racism' has taken on a wider meaning and is now used in a more general way to describe any manifestation of discrimination and prejudice against others on the grounds of race, colour, religion or culture. Such prejudice is more commonplace and widespread than most would like to acknowledge.

In the first section of this chapter I will be looking at the history of racial prejudice and discrimination. Within the nineteenth and twentieth centuries this includes manifestations of racism as defined by modern historians – praxis grounded in racist ideology. Any historical overview is necessarily far from comprehensive. I will be focusing on the history of racism and racial prejudice in the western world and the train of ideological thought that linked their manifestations. The end of this section concentrates specifically on the current situation in the UK. The second section is devoted to a more detailed discussion of the process of racism and racist ideology.

The final section examines the issue of race and culture within counselling and psychotherapy. Perhaps over-optimistically, I would assume racism as an ideology to be absent from these enterprises. However, the issue of response to difference is inevitably present in any contact between two people. Physical differences no less than cultural differences play a part in the counselling and therapeutic relationship. Skin of a different colour may invoke stereotypes that have been absorbed and unchallenged. The culture of both client and therapist will influence how they think, what they value and how they express themselves. Culture and religion may also play a large part in familial and group relationships and in an individual's expectations from interpersonal relationships, including that within the counselling or therapy. To the extent that we are all inevitably part of a culture and possess individual or group values, we are all capable of prejudice and adverse discrimination against someone who seems to be Other.

Racism and racial discrimination – a historical overview

Early history

The classical period appears to be free of racial prejudice based on colour. Both the Greeks and the Romans had a highly positive view of the peoples they encountered whose physical appearance differed significantly from their own. Classical literature contains extensive references to the social, medical and artistic achievements of both the Egyptians and the Ethiopians. Early references to blackness of skin carry no element of judging this as inferior. Skin colour was observed and recorded, but appears to have been no bar to the possibility of co-operation and social acceptance. The Ethiopians inspired respect in both Greeks and Romans; they were viewed as a military power, with their own specific culture. There appears to be no trace of stereotyping blacks as primitive peoples deficient in civilized practices or as physically or morally inferior. Similarly it would seem that the ancients put no premium on racial purity and were unconcerned with degrees of racial mixture.

Colour, therefore, was not an obstacle to integration into society in the Greek and Roman worlds (Snowden, 1983: 63). Both Greek and Roman civilizations, however, did practise slavery, and both held notions viewing their own social institutions and practices and their particular race or group as superior to those they conquered and enslaved. They held strong views about their own perfection, both physically and in terms of the civilizations they had created, and regarded other national groups, for example the Britons, as barbaric, savage and crude. These judgements were based on criteria to do with levels of social and economic development – that is to say cultural rather than racial discrimination. In antiquity slavery as an institution was a fact of life and as such was independent of race or class. The great majority of the thousands of slaves were white, not black. There was no identification of blackness with slavery as developed in later centuries. Such prejudice as did exist in classical times was based on cultural and social evaluations and its impact was insignificant in comparison with the virulent forms of racial prejudice that have emerged in modern times.

The early histories of Judaism, Christianity and Islam are similarly free of prejudice based on colour. Religious intolerance and discrimination were, however, common. Hostility against Jews was inflamed by their refusal to convert to Christianity and by the notion that they were collectively responsible for the Crucifixion. Throughout the medieval period, Jews in Europe were not only socially ostracized but persecuted and killed. Popular mythology associated them with witchcraft and the devil. Jews were blamed for the Black Death in the mid-fourteenth century and thousands were massacred. By this time Jews had acquired pariah status throughout Europe and were isolated from mainstream society – a position they were to occupy for hundreds of years.

The northern European expansion into the African continent led to the beginnings of ideas about the importance of preserving racial purity and the dangers of mixing black and white populations. The first European travellers and explorers to Africa in the fifteenth and sixteenth centuries were the Portuguese. They were interested primarily in trade and wealth and initially there seems to have been assimilation of the Portuguese travellers into the local customs, frequently forming relationships with African women and fathering children. Soon, however, this became a practice that was viewed with disapprobation, particularly by the Catholic Church. What soon emerged was ambivalence between the desire to convert, which was increasingly seen as part of the imperial project, and fear of contamination by the inter-mingling of black and white racial groups.

The English arrived in Africa nearly a century after the Portuguese. They too were initially interested in trade with, rather than the conversion or the conquering of, the natives. Unlike the Portuguese and the Spanish, the English had hitherto had no contact with Africans or dark-skinned peoples. The contrast between the Africans' skin colour and that of the English traveller had a powerful impact on these explorers. They appear to have perceived Africans as a group of people characterized by their difference, in every respect, from the European. Skin colour, religion and life-style all combined to construct a picture of the African as essentially 'other' – unchristian, immodest, libidinous and black. Medieval Christian thought linked blackness with concepts of danger, sin and evil. For the English explorer, therefore, the African was barely human, and clearly at risk of eternal damnation. The assumption of racial superiority by white explorers and settlers was present from the earli-est contact between Europeans and Africans. Indigenous populations were seen as inferior and expendable or, less commonly, as projects for conversion, both to Christianity and the 'civilized' social conventions of the European way of life.

Notions of symbolism associated with blackness and whiteness pre-date the sixteenth century. The polarity of black versus white was linked with filth versus purity, sin versus virginity, evil versus good, ugliness versus beauty, baseness versus virtue. For the Elizabethans, however, whiteness carried a special significance; it was the colour of perfect human beauty, especially female beauty as embod-ied in their fair Queen. As black seamen, servants and slaves began to arrive in Britain the negro became the visual encapsulation of the antithesis of beauty, virtue and purity. The literature of the age reflects these notions. *Othello* encapsulates some of the ambiguities present at the time. While Othello is portrayed as brave and noble, his relationship with a white woman is seen as highly questionable and against the natural order. He is revealed as being uncontrollably emotional, irrational and murderously aggressive – still in fact a barbarian. Fears of black pollution were growing in Britain, and in 1604 Elizabeth I called for the deportation of blacks because their presence in her kingdom was felt to be too great. There are chilling echoes here of events in the mid- to late twentieth century.

Europe in the eighteenth and nineteenth centuries
Most writers on race and racism concur in the view that the foundations for modern racism were laid in the eighteenth century. This is not to say that elements of racist thought and/or behaviour are not discernible earlier, but that there emerged in the period of the Enlightenment and beyond, theories and beliefs which formed a substantial racist ideology. This provided a rationale for racism which had not existed previously. Strains of this ideology are still evident in society today.

George Mosse (1985) traces three strands in eighteenth-century thought which were crucial to the development of this racist ideology. The first was the attempt of the intellectual elite to substitute an emphasis on man's reason for outmoded superstitious ideas. The 'enlightened' rejected Christianity and turned to the classics, the ideals of the Graeco-Roman world, for inspiration. The second strand was Christianity itself, which continued to thrive throughout Europe. Religious fervour and revival created an atmosphere in which great value was given to the emotional life of the 'inner man'; this was viewed as indicative of the state of his spiritual health. The third strand was the growth of natural science and radical attempts to define man's place in nature.

These different strands of thought were intermingled right from the start. Nature and the classics were both seen as essential in understanding man's place in the universe. The new sciences which developed during the century involved studying different groups of men and animals; physical measurements and observations of behaviour formed the basis of comparisons and classifications. The value judgements which accompanied these studies were based on aesthetic criteria derived from Ancient Greece, which was upheld as the epitome of civilization both in its social structures and in the proportions and elements of its sculpture, arts and the people themselves. There was a desire for harmony in the affairs of man; evidence of its existence was taken in the outward form of man himself. Thus we can see the origins of the idea that the outer physical appearance of a human being indicates his inner nature – and not only his personality but his position in society and his very soul.

Throughout the eighteenth century attempts were made to classify nature, beginning with Linnaeus in 1735. Like his predecessors and successors, Linnaeus was influenced by one 'item of intellectual lumber common to educated man' (Curtin, 1965), namely the ancient belief in a 'Great Chain of Being'. This was the idea that all living things fitted into a hierarchy extending from God to man to the smallest animal on earth. Even when (for some) God was removed from the equation, the notion of a hierarchy persisted, carrying with it the assumption that the varieties of mankind too existed in a sequence characterized by higher and lower orders. Linnaeus' first racial classification was based on skin colour with four races: white, red, yellow and black, each located on one of the four major continents. He later modified his classification, and other biologists and ethnologists suggested variants of his thesis. Like Linnaeus, all of the scientists engaged in this field in the eighteenth and nineteenth centuries were European. Not surprisingly when it came to arranging the races in a hierarchy, all of them placed the white European at the top.

In the first half of the eighteenth century Romantic idealism and a desire to forge close links with nature as a route to Christian purity gave rise to the notion of the 'noble savage'. The black man was seen as embodying a primitivism which was unsullied by the corruption of so-called civilization. He was viewed as innocent, charmingly naïve and in tune with the natural elements of his environment. This view was not to last, and as the scientific notions of the age began to dominate popular thought, natives were seen not as uncorrupted by civilization but as lacking in civilization. The image emerged of the black man as lazy, undisciplined, and therefore in need of education and guidance.

By the end of the eighteenth century anthropologists were unanimous in their view that the negro was the lowest link on the great chain of being. Various theories posited that they were closer to the animal world than to the human world, or were halfway between the two, providing the 'missing link' between animals and man. Physical appearance was cited as evidence for these notions along with pseudo-scientific theories based on facial measurements and brain weights. The ideal of classical beauty was used as the prototype for comparison. What emerged from the eighteenth century, therefore, was not only the basis of views about the inherent inferiority of the black man, but notions about the ideals to which the superior race was supposed to conform. Within these ideas the connection between outward physical appearance and inner moral and intellectual characteristics was firmly established.

At the beginning of the nineteenth century there was still much debate about why the peoples of the world differed so much in their physical appearance. Michael Banton (1997) summarizes the contemporary explanations into four possible answers. The first was based on the Bible. We are all descended from Adam and Eve and God had placed a curse on the descendants of Ham, making them black. Variations of this theory posited Shem and Japhet, Ham's brothers, as founders of other distinct racial groups. The second answer was environmental. Living in tropical climates had the effect of turning the skin black. The third answer was close to Darwinian theory; accidental variations are selectively preserved because of environmental or other factors. As this ran counter to the teachings of the Bible it seemed at the time unlikely as well as unpopular. The fourth answer was the one that gained ascendancy, supported as it was by the developing science of anthropology. This was the idea that the world was divided into a series of natural provinces. There is a finite number of permanent human types, each with its own set of distinct characteristics. The theory of 'racial typology' was significant because it asserted that the different human groups were distinct species rather than varieties of the same species. Proponents of this theory believed that the pure human types were permanent and unchanging and that if there was (ill-advised) mixing between different groups, the hybrid lines would die out.

As theories of 'scientific racism' developed, the belief that whites were naturally superior to other races was reinforced by citation of their achievements as evidence of such. It was suggested that one of the characteristics of the white race was that of being ideally suited to develop and colonize other, less endowed, areas of the world. Thus the difference between whites and blacks was not just one of different stages of advancement, but stemmed from an innate and permanent superiority of white over black. These views were supported by a spate of pseudo-scientific studies measuring and comparing such things as the 'facial angle', the shape of the skull (phrenology) or the weight of the brain, all of which purported to demonstrate the inferiority of the black and coloured races and the superiority of the whites. As physical characteristics were indications of other aspects of the human personality, racial type was seen as an immutable indicator of such things as intelligence, morality, inventiveness, orderliness and so on – that is to say the values of the white middle-class nineteenth-century European.

The most exhaustive exposition of racial typology was provided by Arthur de Gobineau in his book *Essay on the Inequality of the Human Races* (1853–4). Gobineau classified man into three races: yellow, black and white. The black race was seen as the lowest and was assigned characteristics by now traditional in racial thought: limited intelligence, animality and over-developed sensual desires, inability to distinguish between vice and virtue, horrific impassiveness to suffering, and a crude and terrifying energy. The yellow race, he believed, was materialistic, pedantic, apathetic and lacking in physical strength. It was seen as mediocre and with weak desires. The white race, however, embodied the virtues of nobility, love of freedom, honour, spirituality, perseverance, physical power and superior intelligence. Gobineau believed that the mixing of the races was sadly inevitable but that over time this would lead to the degeneration and eventual disappearance of racial purity. Many of Gobineau's ideas, in particular the notion of blood purity, were taken up and used by theorists who followed. As Biddiss states, 'the subsequent treatment of Gobineau's theory was far from what he intended, and he became the inventor of twentieth century racism rather by accident' (Biddiss, 1966). Gobineau's thesis was taken up by German thinkers and there is a clear line of intellectual thought from here to Hitler.

In a similar way the theories of Charles Darwin were adopted by racial theoreticians. It is easy to see how concepts like 'natural selection' and 'survival of the fittest' could be diverted for such use. Darwin's ideas were complex and placed emphasis on the environment as the main factor in the variation of species. His followers changed this emphasis to one of heredity, which led to a focus on the inherent qualities of racial stock. Francis Galton, a follower of Darwin, dominated European research into heredity, and in his work *Hereditary Genius* (1869) he laid the foundations of the eugenics movement. Here we find the chilling notions that the birth rate of the unfit should be checked and that of the fit encouraged through early marriage. It was a short step from here to the idea that those considered unfit (because of undesirable characteristics which were innate in their racial type) should not only not be allowed to reproduce, but should be exterminated, for reasons of 'racial hygiene'.

As is so often the case, the events of a period lag behind the developing intellectual thought. During the latter part of the eighteenth and the beginning of the nineteenth centuries, Europe experienced a period of democratic revolution and liberal humanism. The Enlightenment and the French Revolution promoted ideas which emphasized the shared characteristics and fundamental equality of all humankind. The position of Jews and other oppressed minorities improved significantly in most European countries during this time. This movement was echoed in the New World, where slaves were emancipated in 1863 and the Fourteenth Amendment (1868) granted equal citizenship for all born in the USA. The civil and political emancipation of the Jews took place throughout Europe between 1789 and 1871. Prior to this, Jews had been set apart from Christians in Europe by special taxes, residential restrictions, public stigmatization and limited civil status and autonomy. However, their reprieve was short-lived and from the 1870s onwards there was a significant backlash against such liberal ideas. The ideologies that had been developing since the beginning of the eighteenth century were brought into play as scientific racism constructed absolute boundaries between the races based on notions of fixed biological differences (MacMaster, 2001: 16).

USA and slavery

Slavery has existed in many forms throughout recorded history – and not only of black or coloured groups of people. It has historically been regarded as a justifiable way of treating those you have conquered in battle. By virtue of being defeated, the conquered race, group or nation is demonstrably less strong; slavery is also an effective way of subjugating any residue of resistance. Slavery was practised in America for almost 200 years. American slaves, however, were not the subjects of a nation defeated in battle. They were human beings specifically captured and sold to provide lifelong, and very economical, labour in a country short of manpower. Slaves imported from Africa were a commodity whose transportation and sale provided a livelihood for traders, as well as meeting the economic and labour needs of the New World.

In examining the history of slavery in America there is a circular debate among historians as to which came first, slavery or racism. In other words, were blacks enslaved because they were viewed as inferior, or was the theory of their inferiority invented to justify slavery? This debate is based on the distinction between societal racism and ideological racism. As we have seen in Europe, there is considerable evidence of racism existing in the social treatment of minority groups well before the ideology that developed in the eighteenth and nineteenth centuries. In many ways the history of America over the same period mirrors this pattern. The theories about race that emerged during this time were useful to many whites in America in providing a 'scientific' rationale for their behaviour and practices.

According to Fredrickson (1988), the English colonists brought with them to the New World a predisposition towards colour prejudice as a result of England's early contacts with Africa. Blackness was associated with savagery, heathenness and a general lack of civilized behaviour. There was also the age-old association of black with evil. The unfavourable black stereotype already existed by the seventeenth century. Blacks were first introduced to Virginia as 'servants' between 1619 and 1640, and by the 1660s slavery was legally sanctioned. By the early eighteenth century the development of a slave plantation economy saw the introduction of laws banning intermarriage between blacks and whites and forbidding private manumission. Blacks were deprived of all rights granted to whites and a rigid social classification sanctioned the treatment of blacks in ways which were in many instances inhumane and brutal.

A racist ideology did not fully develop in America until the nineteenth century when we see an emergence of theoretical concepts similar to those in Europe. The environmentalist view of the eighteenth century, however, had significant impact in parts of America. The idea that racial characteristics were not innate but rather the result of environmental factors, combined with the natural-rights philosophy, led to an attack on the institution of slavery in the north during the era of the American Revolution. This precipitated the beginning of emancipation in the northern states. However, following the Declaration of Independence, abolitionist feeling forced pro-slavery southerners to refine and articulate a racist theory to defend their treatment of black slaves. The expression of this theory in America was focused on black groups, whereas in Europe it became the cornerstone of anti-Semitism. In the American South both personal wealth and the social structures in place were dependent on the slave economy and the maintenance of the negro's inferior status. In the northern states, where slaves had been emancipated after the Revolution, blacks were subjected to segregation, discrimination and violence. Following general emancipation anti-black racism reached horrific heights. Blacks were frequently hanged or burnt alive by lynch mobs and the popular view was of the black man as a vicious brutal beast who needed to be kept in his place.

Emancipation could not be carried to completion because it was impossible for the white American, in the North as well as the South, to think of blacks as genuine equals. As Fredrickson (2002: 81) puts it: 'efforts to extend the meaning of emancipation to include black civil and political equality awakened the demons of racism to a greater extent than the polemical defense of slavery had done'. Thus the Civil War resulted in the emancipation of the negro from slavery but not from caste discrimination and the ravages of racism. The civil rights movement in the USA, which gained momentum after the Second World War, succeeded in finally outlawing legalized racial segregation and discrimination in the 1960s. This movement benefited from a feeling of revulsion against the Holocaust as the logical extreme of racism. Following the Second World War scientific racism lost its credibility, although societal racism and racial discrimination persisted in the USA as in Europe.

Europe in the twentieth century
In the early years of the twentieth century there was mass migration of non-white peoples from the third world to the industrial societies of the first world. This led to social unease in many places, and in Britain the right of free entry to the country was restricted by the Aliens Acts of 1905 and 1919. Those immigrants who settled in Britain encountered widespread prejudice which adversely affected their opportunities in key areas such as employment and housing. Surveys of the time portray this group as a social-pathological minority; on the whole they remained isolated in the worst social and economic conditions. The mainstream of English racial prejudice centred upon the black, because of Britain's imperial past. On the continent, however, racial discrimination became focused on the Jews.

Anti-Semitic feeling had been present in Germany before unification. The movement towards a unified German state was based on the concept of national membership defined by ethnic origins rather than human rights. The German philosopher Johann Gottfried von Herder (1744–1803) had propounded the theory that each ethnic group possesses a unique *Volksgeist* (folk soul) which should be protected from contamination. Jews were seen as a source of such contamination. However, broader libertarian attitudes throughout Europe in the nineteenth century led widely to the emancipation of the Jews. This allowed German Jews to participate in their country's prosperity in the latter part of this century. Despite this, deep-seated racial prejudice, combined with German nationalism and fears of Jews over-running those of pure German descent, led to overt expressions of anti-Semitism by the turn of the century. It was the Nazis who combined these powerful feelings with scientific racism to such devastating effect.

The eugenics movement, begun in the late nineteenth century, gave rise in the early twentieth century to the doctrine of 'racial and social biology'. Any racial mixing was seen as dangerous, leading to 'degeneracy'. The black race was still seen as innately inferior, but by the mid-1930s the negative characteristics which had for so long been attributed solely to the blacks were also assigned to the Jewish race. The desire to preserve racial purity meant that eugenics must be practised by the superior race to keep it from degeneration and the threat of extinction. The 'unfit', that is those belonging to a lesser race or those damaged by disease or disability, should at the very least be sterilized but preferably eliminated. The history of Nazism and Hitler's implementation of anti-Semitism is well documented. But it is vital to see the Holocaust in the context of the racial ideology that had been developing in the preceding 150 years. The Nazis were only carrying to a logical conclusion the racist opinions and doctrines that held sway throughout

Europe and America before the Second World War. As a result an estimated 5,933,900 Jews and other ethnic minorities were killed.

In his analysis of European racism, George Mosse stresses the continuity of thought in racial stereotypes from the early eighteenth century to the Holocaust. The stereotypes of beauty and ugliness remained the same, as did the crucial notion of the outward appearance of a man mirroring the workings of his inner nature.

> From the eighteenth century to its use by the Nazis in the holocaust, this stereotype never changed. The virile, Hellenistic type juxtaposed with the dark and misshapen villain, the Aryan of Greek proportions versus the ill-proportioned Jew, made racism a visually centred ideology. (Mosse, 1985: 233)

Racism, however, did not die out with the Holocaust. Notions of ideological racism, racial biology and eugenics were largely discredited in the aftermath of the Second World War. Many, however, have re-emerged with different labels – 'ethnic cleansing' being the most recent. The post-war world was very sensitive about any expressions of anti-Semitism, but this sensitivity did not spread to the blacks. Countries which had fought to defeat Hitler and National Socialism continued to accept black racial inferiority for many years after the war, while being vociferous in their condemnation of Nazi racism. Racist ideology was central, for example, to the implementation of apartheid in South Africa. Established in 1948, this regime restricted Africans, more than 70 per cent of the total population, to approximately 13 per cent of the total land area of South Africa. Blacks and whites were segregated in all areas of life, with intermarriage forbidden. The aim of this regime, like others before it, was white supremacy based on an ideology of innate black inferiority.

When we look at the history of racial ideology, what emerges quite clearly is that ideas of racial difference and the notions of inferiority and superiority that go with them existed long before they were underpinned by pseudo-scientific theory. They have continued to exist long after such theories have been discredited.

Britain after the Second World War

The history of racism and racial ideas in the period from 1945 to the present day is characterized by a move from racial difference as the justification for overt racist behaviour based on assumptions about superiority and inferiority, to an ideology where racial difference is 'celebrated' as in notions of multiculturalism and cultural pluralism. While there is no doubt that in general the position and social treatment of black and coloured people has improved immeasurably since the 1930s, it is also the case that racism has continued to be manifested in all areas of society. It is undeniable too that many white Britons, because of the prevailing liberal ideas of 'multiculturalism' professed by the media, have an image of their country and of themselves as being tolerant, accepting and free of prejudice, an image which is very far from being true.

In the period following the end of the Second World War, most of Britain's colonies in Africa, Asia and the Caribbean came to experience full independence at approximately the same time. Partly because of this there were large groups of peoples who migrated from these areas to Britain between the late 1940s and the 1970s. Prior to this Britain had seen itself as a white country. But this was no longer feasible by the 1960s when the ideology of multiculturalism began to emerge. Up until this point the prevailing assumption had been that any newcomers would be assimilated into the dominant culture. This assumption was easier to maintain when those entering the country were less visible – as with Irish, Poles, Germans and other Europeans who moved to Britain in the nineteenth and twentieth centuries. With the advent of large groups of black and coloured people, the idea of assimilation became more problematic. This was not only because there continued to be resistance to inter-marriage between people of different colours (by both blacks and whites) but also because the immigrants them-selves in many instances maintained ties with their coun-tries of origin and showed no desire to relinquish their own customs and cultural practices. On the contrary, by the 1960s many minority racial groups were uniting in a call for racial cohesion and pride in their own cultural heritage, as well as demanding greater representation in all areas of British life. It is significant that in Britain the word 'immi-grant' has come to mean people who enter the country *and* who are black or brown. This takes no account of the vast numbers of arrivals who are white. Indeed in the 1980s there were more white than black immigrants.

The political focus that began in the 1950s and contin-ues to the present day has been on how to control or cur-tail immigration. A series of Acts, beginning with the Immigration Act in 1971, have attempted to limit entry by various means. What these various pieces of legislation demonstrate is the ever-present resistance to the entry of black people to the UK. There is a fear, rarely articulated but occasionally hinted at, that a relaxation of control of immigration by blacks will lead to a situation where whites are no longer in the majority. At the same time there has been a political and social awareness of the need to fight racial discrimination as evidenced by the three Race Relations Acts (1965, 1968 and 1976). The counterpoise between the exclusionary nationality and immigration laws and the anti-discriminatory legislation seems to imply an underlying principle that more immigration would be inimical to good race relations in Britain. Significantly the 1976 Race Relations Act heralded a shift in emphasis, pro-mulgating the notion of a multicultural society in which there should be no attempt to achieve integration through assimilation, but through promoting mutual tolerance within diversity. This Act made discrimination unlawful on grounds of race, colour, nationality and ethnic or national origin.

Throughout the second half of the twentieth century, and into the twenty-first century, there has been continual racial tension in the UK, erupting periodically into riots, mob violence and countless individual incidents of racially motivated attacks of varying severity. Many commentators point to the legislation on immigration as a source of exacerbating the existing problem by creating, or reinforcing, an image of black and Asian immigrants as a social problem – in other words stigmatizing and stereotyping these groups. At various times resistance to immigration and explicit racist thought have crystallized around specific groups. The National Front in 1967 emphasized in their programme the need to preserve 'our British Native Stock' by 'terminating non-white immigration' (Holmes, 1991: 57). In 1968 Enoch Powell delivered his infamous 'Rivers of Blood' speech, spawning for a time the movement of Powellism. In the late twentieth century the British National Party has been increasingly active. Their use of the Union flag as an emblem is symptomatic of their belief in British nationalism as an exclusively white prerogative.

The contemporary situation
The Commission for Racial Equality, set up in 1976 to enforce the Race Relations Act, has been active in monitoring the situation in all areas of life throughout the UK. Despite this, their current findings are depressing. Ethnic minorities are three times more likely than whites to be homeless and five times more likely to be living in poor or overcrowded conditions (CRE, 1999a). There is still a disproportionate number of ethnic minorities engaged in unskilled and low-paid jobs, and black and Asian men are twice as likely to be unemployed as white men – in London

and some other inner-city areas this figure rises to three times as likely (CRE, 1999b). The 1996 Ofsted report showed that Afro-Caribbean boys are excluded from school up to six times more frequently than their white counterparts for similar behaviour. Since then both exclusion rates and the disproportionate exclusion of children from ethnic minorities have risen. Those young people from ethnic minority groups who do achieve good educational qualifications (more commonly Asian than Afro-Caribbean children) experience more difficulty than their white counterparts in securing employment.

Efforts to become part of the political body have also been largely unsuccessful – black and Asian groups are grossly under-represented politically. In 1998 there were twelve non-white MPs in the House of Commons. In order to reflect a percentage of the population this figure should be fifty (CRE, 1999b). A 1994 Home Office report found that each year there are between 89,000 and 171,000 racially motivated incidents such as assaults, threats or vandalism directed against Asians or Afro-Caribbeans. The police and justice systems have increasingly come under public scrutiny, particularly since the murder of Stephen Lawrence in 1993 and that of Damilola Taylor in 2001. The inquiry following Stephen Lawrence's death brought acknowledgement from the British government, for the first time, that institutional racism exists in the police force. Despite that, an undercover operation by a journalist in October 2003 exposed racist beliefs and behaviour in members of the Greater Manchester police force, leading to the resignation of several police officers. The fact remains, however, that black and brown people are far more likely to be the victims of attacks on the streets or in their homes than are white people. Furthermore, black men are eight times more likely to be stopped and searched by the police than white men, Asian men being three times more likely. So, despite repeated legislation and high levels of social awareness, black and Asian groups in the UK continue to encounter racism and discrimination in all areas of their lives. Meanwhile the vast majority of the white population have succeeded in retaining an image of themselves, individually, as non-racist. A survey conducted in 1984 revealed that 90 per cent of the survey sample believed that blacks and Asians in Britain met with prejudice. However, 64 per cent of the respondents placed themselves in the 'not prejudiced at all' category and only 4 per cent admitted to being 'very prejudiced' (Holmes, 1991: 3). An opinion poll conducted in 1995 came up with similar results; the term 'pluralistic ignorance' has been coined to describe this phenomenon.

From the late 1980s there has been a growing hostility in Britain, as elsewhere, towards Muslims, generated by fears of Islamic fundamentalism. Following the horrific events of 11 September 2001, there have been many violent incidents, both in Europe and the USA, against people who are perceived (correctly or incorrectly) to be Muslim. The identification of an individual as belonging to a particular ethnic group by their appearance (colour of skin, or their manner of dress – in this instance wearing a turban) can lead to the assumption that the individual shares the attitudes and views of other members of the group who have committed acts of violence. This process – the assumption of homogeneity in all aspects of personality and life-style because of *one* shared aspect – is common to all forms of prejudice and discrimination and is particularly pernicious for those who are its recipients. In the current climate it is potentially dangerous or even life-threatening for many Muslims residing in Europe or the USA. Intense sensitivity and controversy over immigration into the UK has been revived since 11 September; in the media and public consciousness 'asylum seeker' has become almost synonymous with 'terrorist suspect'.

Fredrickson (2002: 145) suggests that what we are witnessing is a process whereby culture and religion are being essentialized to a point where they serve as the functional equivalent of biological racism – in other words a person's faith or culture is judged to be an unchangeable and potentially threatening element of who they are, and has become the grounds on which it is justifiable to discriminate against or persecute him or her. He posits the possibility of the colour line of the twentieth century being replaced or overshadowed by the faith or creed lines of the twenty-first century (ibid.: 148). The social and political events of the current century do nothing to refute such a view.

Meanwhile, theories which underpin a racist ideology have never completely gone away. E.O. Wilson's theories of sociobiology (1975) led to a resurgence in ideas of biological determinism, which have been used as justification by racist movements such as the National Front. Wilson's claims that territoriality, tribalism and xenophobia are part of the human genetic constitution have been taken up by such organizations in their crusade for maintaining Britain as an exclusively white nation and as a justification for their attacks on blacks and Asians residing in Britain. Carter (1995: 32) cites a number of contemporary scholars (zoologists, social scientists and anthropologists) whose theories of racial topology and inferiority, based on skeletal morphology, hair, facial features, head size and genetic structure are strikingly similar to the writers of the eighteenth and nineteenth centuries. Like their predecessors, these modern theorists are not simply pointing out differences between racial groups, but are implying a comparative standard of better and worse, with whites portrayed as superior to blacks. In *The Bell Curve*, published in 1994, Herrnstein and Murray claimed to show that whites are superior in intelligence to blacks and other people of colour. These ideas seem to resurface regularly and are widely disseminated through media reports, provoking a chorus of voices and research that challenges and rejects such thinking. What we are seeing here is a manifestation of the confusion between different and better/worse. Theories that attempt to highlight possible differences between racial groups are quickly adopted and (if necessary) distorted by some to 'prove' white racial superiority. In order to 'disprove' such assertions it is seen as imperative to insist on total equality of biological endowment.

It would seem that despite a widespread growth in liberal ideas since the Second World War, a general recognition of the importance of equality and acceptance within society, and the establishment of humanitarian movements and organizations which reject, intellectually at least, the old ideologies of superiority/inferiority based on colour and race, prejudice and racial discrimination have never ceased to exist. In any situation of stress – competition for jobs, housing or advantage; incidents of violence or sexual attacks involving people of different racial groups or different skin colour; situations which threaten national security – old stereotypes have surfaced anew and the likelihood of the presence of racism is high. Some socialist theorists believe that antipathy towards minority groups is an inevitable consequence of capitalism (Holmes, 1991: 85). In some respects this appears to be borne out by history – as societies have become industrialized, more complex and more economically sophisticated, racial disharmony has become an increasingly predominant feature within them. A factor of greater significance, however, would appear to be the movement of groups of people made possible by the technological developments of the nineteenth and twentieth centuries. As soon as different racial groups live side by side within the same social structure, rather than separated by geographical distance, hostility and prejudice inevitably surface. The potential for the expression of that hostility towards minorities appears to reside in all societies, and in all individuals within those societies.

The process of racism and racial discrimination

To what extent is adverse discrimination against another person or group on the grounds of their race or cultural practices a phenomenon rooted in human nature, and to what extent is it the product of particular historical or social circumstances? As we have seen, the typologists believed that each racial type inherited not only physical but also psychological characteristics. Each type was also believed to inherit innate attitudes towards members of other races. Thus racial prejudice was believed to be an inherited disposition. This view was challenged with the development of psychological research and environmental theories which claimed that racial prejudice was learned in the course of a child's upbringing. The kind of inherited psychology suggested by the typologists – that the white races are naturally superior, leaders and colonizers, and the black races are naturally inferior and subservient, has been widely discredited, not the least because of its obvious racist undertones. But, as we have seen, there does seem to be some human disposition to fear the Other, which is aroused in a particularly virulent way by difference in skin colour, and which can manifest itself in the form of prejudice and racial discrimination.

Central to the debate about the origins of racist manifestations and regimes and to discussions around the use of terminology such as 'racism', 'ethnocentricism', 'xenophobia', and the like, is an attempt to distinguish between that element of a prejudiced or 'racist' response which stems from a person's individual psychology and that element which has its origin in generally consensual group or social attitudes. At the heart of this are questions about both individual and group or 'generally human' psychology, and how the two interact. In addressing these issues, it would be useful to examine the different ideas, concepts and psychological mechanisms that underlie the process whereby racism, racial discrimination and racial prejudice are manifested. Some of these elements can be traced back historically – they have their roots in the history of racial thought, as already outlined. Others are specific to a particular time, place or social group.

Black/white symbolism

The association of white with good and black with evil, and all the related connotations, pertains particularly to the western tradition. It found its apotheosis in Christianity, but there is no doubt that it existed before. White stands for purity, joy, beauty, health, virginity, cleanliness, virtue; black stands for negation, disorder, defilement, ugliness, illness, corruption, filth, and so on. In literature and art the symbolism is carried further – they are symbols of two opposing universes and irreconcilable opposites; day and night, renunciation and sensuality, culture and nature, life and death, God and the devil.

In non-western cultures there does not appear, historically, to be the same black/white imagery. In Africa black may represent something auspicious or benevolent. In classical Chinese opera, black-painted faces represent integrity, white faces evil. However, one of the effects of the colonial period on many parts of the world appears to have been to import the connotations of white as superior. Following the abolition of slavery and the end of colonial rule, the Christian missions perpetuated the idea that blacks could achieve an 'inner whiteness' by conversion to the Christian faith. This would 'wash away' their sins if not their outer blackness, and allow them to be saved from the damnation to which the blackness of their souls otherwise condemned them.

We still apply a more or less strict division between black and white when talking about racial groups. This distinction applies despite the presence of mixed-race relationships and the fact that people of mixed-race descent are an increasing proportion of society. And it applies despite the fact that differences of complexion constitute a continuous distribution, from very dark to very light, with varying shades of brown, yellow and pink between. In the United States, in particular, there is a rigid white/black classification. This is the result of what is known as the 'one-drop rule', which has its origins in the ideology propounded to justify black slavery. According to the one-drop rule a person is racially black if he or she has one black ancestor anywhere in his or her genealogical line of descent, and regardless of how many white, Asian or native American ancestors are involved. By contrast a person is white only if he or she has no non-white ancestors. The one-drop rule is still public policy in the USA and has the effect of perpetrating not only the black-is-bad, white-is-good symbolism but also the ideas of racial or 'blood' purity and the fears of contamination which had such catastrophic consequences in Europe in the 1940s. Recent results from the Human Genome Project have found that humans are 99.9 per cent alike, and scientists in this field have been quick to refute the idea that race has a genetic or scientific basis. However, genetic testing is able to identify specific 'markers' which are indicative of ethnic origin, and one scientist has estimated that people who are considered black in America are on average 20 per cent Caucasian (Griffith, 2002). What is striking is that, despite such findings, people are universally judged on their *appearance* of colour, with dark skins being less desirable than light ones.

Many commentators have drawn attention to one of the more insidious effects of black/white symbolism and the ideas of innate inferiority/superiority associated with it: the adoption of these ideas by blacks themselves with the result that they too begin to place greater value on lightness of skin colour. Virginia Harris calls this phenomenon 'colorism'; it is particularly noticeable in the Caribbean and some parts of Latin America, where those people with lighter skins are assigned greater status, are more sought after as marriage partners, and those with darker skins suffer greater deprivation due to discrimination. Harris ascribes this phenomenon also to African Americans and cites evidence of the same prejudice operating in China and the Philippines (Harris, 1998: 67). Yasmin Alibhai-Brown draws attention to the effects of this complex in Britain, where she notes a tendency among successful black and Asian men to choose white partners 'almost as the finishing touches to their impressive cvs' (Alibhai-Brown, 2001: 13). The implications here are clear: to be accepted by the majority culture you need to become like them in as many ways as possible. This may mean denying your own race and colour. To succeed you need to assimilate, regardless of the costs. In this way racism can become internalized within black and coloured people as part of their inner world as well as present in their external reality.

Stereotyping

We have seen how the strands of intellectual thought in the eighteenth and nineteenth centuries gave birth to racial stereotypes based on classical ideals of beauty. The black stereotype was that of an inferior group, incapable of being civilized, lacking in the virtues exemplified by the superior white races. The black man was seen as a savage, first noble, then barbaric. He was stereotyped as immoral, dishonest, unclean, lazy, with limited intelligence or potential for intellectual development. The advantage of this kind of attitude (for those in the superior group) is that it gives everyone a designated place, and one which is immutable. If these characteristics are not susceptible to change (because they are inherited, or are indicative of belonging to a particular racial 'type', or whatever theory holds sway at the time) then the social order is fixed – and not by anything as potentially guilt-provoking as exploitation.

A similar process has been a central part of anti-Semitism. Jews have always been stereotyped as evil and corrupt, unscrupulous and cunning. Like the black man in the nineteenth century, the Jew was characterized as lacking in physical beauty and grace – as the epitome of ugliness. This was to lead to the fateful contrast between the Jew and the Aryan. With both the Jew and the black, fear of contamination by intermarriage has produced the stereotype of the sexual predator – the black or the Jew who preys on white women and will thus violate racial boundaries and dilute the 'purity' of the white race.

The black stereotype has in particular been associated with notions of physical power, violent tendencies, sexual prowess and attractiveness, uncontrollable lust. Many of these stereotypes persist today. Black and mixed-race women are still viewed as being exotic, erotic and morally suspect (Zack, Shrage and Sartwell, 1998: 82); Asian women are seen as 'submissive' and black women as 'whores' (Alibhai-Brown, 2001: 10). The attack or sexual assault of a white woman or man by blacks arouses a greater degree of public moral outrage than that accorded to white rapists or non-white victims. By the same token black men are far more likely to be imprisoned for acts of assault than white men committing a similar offence.

In writing about racism in the early twentieth century Mosse says, 'the mental and physical characteristics attributed to these outsiders reflected the fears of society: restlessness, lust and sloth' (Mosse, 1985: xiv). This is a process which continues. We not only attribute to the outsider the fears of society as a whole, but perhaps also those parts of ourselves which we fear to acknowledge – our aggression and our sexual desires.

Fear
The idea that we project onto others the impulses we find unacceptable in ourselves is of course a notion grounded in psychoanalytic theory. Combined with ideas of white/black imagery it constitutes a powerful argument for the explanation of racial discrimination. The black becomes the dirty, hidden, unacknowledged, repressed part of ourselves we would prefer not to own – the shadow, the dark part of the self. The frustrations engendered by 'normal' social and personal difficulties often seek to be released by aggression.

Displaced aggression is easier to cope with because we are then able to maintain our own image of ourselves as decent, moral, clean, honest, and so on. By projecting onto the Other our unacknowledged impulses and desires and then attacking the Other for possessing such undesirable elements, we are, in effect, killing two psychological birds with one stone. If we accept this theory we have to accept that every white person has a personal and individual responsibility for racism.

Littlewood and Lipsedge (1989) draw attention to certain dangers inherent in the psychoanalytic approach. The principal one is that it ignores any historical or social context. Racism comes to be located solely within each individual and is re-invented, as it were, in each person's lifetime. No account is given of why in a particular society at a particular time racism exists and functions. Similarly, no cognizance is given to the powerful and undeniable cumulative effects of intellectual thought over a period of time. However, it would seem that whatever the particular historical circumstances that give rise to racism, there has to be something within each individual which responds to the call. Our potential to be judgemental and discriminatory, our tendency to self-deception about unacceptable aggressive or sexual impulses may, under the right conditions, erupt in hostility towards the perceived 'Other'. Racism is thus a combination of external and internal factors.

There is no doubt that fear plays a part in racism. This can take many forms: irrational fear of the unknown, the different, the Other. Fear perhaps of part of ourselves as represented by the Other, or projected onto that person or group unconsciously; fear of 'contamination' – that our society might be undermined by inter-racial contact, that our dominant 'white' culture will be weakened or cease to be the prevailing one; fear of being overwhelmed by the other race. At times when such fears are activated and appear to have the potential to be translated into reality, racism is at its most intense. The incarceration of Japanese residents in the USA towards the end of the Second World War is an example of this. Similarly, racial violence has erupted in Britain at times when an influx of immigrants has created greater competition for employment and housing. Such rational explanations do not, however, account for the vehemence of feeling engendered in such events. Part of the response produced by fear is the global identification of all members of a race or group as being the cause, or potential cause, of a particular incident or perceived threat. This was painfully evident in the aftermath of the events of 11 September 2001, when Muslims throughout the western world were attacked indiscriminately.

Attribution of racial group identity
One of the most striking, and indeed inescapable, elements of race is the visibility of racial characteristics. This is of course particularly true of the coloured races. As we have seen, in Britain's history black and Asian groups who have entered the country at various times have found integration virtually impossible, while non-coloured immigrant groups have met with fewer difficulties.

Accounts by black writers of their experiences in a predominantly white society focus again and again on the experience of being defined by their skin colour. As Fanon puts it: 'I am overdetermined from without. I am the slave, not of the "idea" that others have of me but of my own appearance' (Fanon, 1986: 116). Many prejudgements about individuals are based on outward differences such as skin colour or mode of dress. We are usually assigned by others to a racial group on sight. It thus becomes an involuntary classification over which we have no control, and a process which can exert a lot of pressure upon individuals to identify themselves with the group to which they have been assigned.

Identity as part of a group is an important part not only of our individual psychology but also of our social survival.

We are all part of many different groups by virtue of our gender, social class, race, educational achievement, economic status, religious beliefs, and so on. The difficulty arises when we are assigned to a group by others by virtue of a characteristic we possess over which we have no control *and* when that characteristic becomes the main or sole element by which we are identified. This is very often the case with race and particularly with black or coloured racial groups. A black person is not only never invisible in a predominantly white society, but his blackness can have the effect of blinding others to any other part of who he is.

Group identity as part of a race also carries with it, as we have seen, assumptions by others of collective responsibility for any act carried out by that race. In this way individual identity is not only reduced to one element of a person's whole being, but that reduced identity is then subsumed into a larger group with an assumption of homogeneity and collective action. Common sense tells us that all members of any racial group are not homogeneous. To assume that they are further diminishes our understanding of each individual within that group.

Political correctness
Social activism, which began slowly in the middle of the twentieth century and gained momentum in the 1970s, has led to a shift from overt expressions of racial beliefs to more covert manifestations. Expressions of racial prejudice are suppressed, disguised or distorted as they have become socially unacceptable in most western countries. The emphasis on 'political correctness' in our use of language in particular is seen by many as a defensive attempt to hide, or deny the existence of racism. It is by no means an indication that racism has ceased to exist – simply that we should take special care not to articulate such beliefs. By adopting a stance of 'colour blindness' in this way, many people school themselves to act as if there is no such thing as

race. My colour and your colour must not be mentioned, least of all as in any way having an impact on the way the two of us interact. This is particularly so if we happen to be in possession of different skin colours. This stance is clearly as nonsensical as identifying someone solely by the colour of their skin. Denying that their race is part of their (many-faceted and complex) identity is equally dehumanizing. As Goulbourne points out, such a stance is the luxury of those in the majority group:

> groups and individuals placed on the deficit side of the racial or colour-line can have little sympathy with the absurdities of the supposed colour blindness on the part of those who, structurally if not through individual choice, benefit from being placed on the privileged side of the colour-line. (Goulbourne, 1998: ix)

Furthermore, political correctness can have the effect of inhibiting discussion and debate about racial prejudice, both internally within each of us individually and within the wider social context.

Racial minority groups in our society continue to be disadvantaged, and the conclusion is inescapable that this is, at least partly, due to racial discrimination. To pretend that it does not exist is not only socially irresponsible, but contributes to the perpetuation of the very thing we are trying to ignore. Attempts to be 'politically correct', to ignore race as a factor in interpersonal, social or political relationships can lead to the emergence of a response which can be both patronizing and paternalistic. It contains within it the enduring idea of white superiority: we must not victimize those who are less developed, less able, less intelligent. We must help the oppressed and disadvantaged, not because we are their oppressors but because they are in need of our help due to their inherent deficits. This attitude too has a long history both in the anti-slavery movement and in social activism in the nineteenth century. It is insidious and difficult to combat because of its seemingly benign public face. It is encapsulated in the sentence 'I am not racist; some of my best friends are black.' But at the heart of this kind of paternalism is the normative ideology that the inferior races should be kept in their place.

Race and culture in counselling and psychotherapy

The relationship between black and coloured groups and the mental health professions in Britain has long been recognized to be problematic. In the UK there is a disproportionately high incidence of Afro-Caribbean men being diagnosed as mentally ill and being compulsorily admitted to an institution under the Mental Health Act. At the same time black and ethnic minorities are significantly under-represented as clients in the fields of counselling and psychotherapy. Very few psychiatrists, psychotherapists and counsellors come from these groups. The obvious conclusion to draw is that racial discrimination is at work in this area. It would be useful, however, to examine further the background to this state of affairs, and to assess the different theories offered as to why this should be so.

Psychiatry

The development of psychiatric theory in the twentieth century was heavily influenced by the beliefs in racial inferiority that flourished in the nineteenth century. Biological determinism had been a very useful doctrine to justify colonialism, slavery and economic exploitation. Black slaves were seen as psychologically adjusted if they were content with their subservient position; to protest or rebel was taken as a sign of mental disorder. Following emancipation, studies of mental illness frequently focused on the differences between whites and blacks, with the assumption that the latter had a less developed, or inherently inferior, psychological and mental state, and were therefore more prone to insanity. The early mental institutions in the USA were segregated on racial lines; the belief was that different races had different psychologies and therefore required different forms of treatment. By the 1950s in the USA and Europe, changes in the social and political climate led scholars to acknowledge the existence of racial discrimination and social oppression. Different theories have been offered to explain psychological disturbance in black and coloured people.

It is disturbing to note, however, that the view that black people are more disturbed and more prone to mental illness than white people still persists – and not only among psychiatrists. Carter cites a study by E.E. Jones in 1982 in which black and white therapists assessed the treatment and outcome of black and white clients. Jones found that white therapists tended to evaluate black clients as significantly more psychologically disturbed than white clients. Black therapists' evaluations did not support this bias (Carter, 1995: 160).

Many studies have been conducted to examine mental illness in immigrant groups. The findings uphold the perception that immigrants are more likely to be treated for psychiatric disorders than non-immigrants. Various hypotheses have been put forward to explain this: that vulnerable people are more likely to emigrate, or that the processes of emigration, immigration and adjustment are themselves potentially psychologically damaging and therefore likely to cause mental illness. The term 'culture shock' was coined to describe the processes experienced by people moving to a different country and culture. This may have gone some way to highlighting the inner experiences of immigrant groups – psychological strain, loss, rejection, anxiety and so forth – but it took no account of the external reality of prejudice and racial discrimination. However, while many of these theories hold water for first-generation immigrants, they should not apply to subsequent generations, of which there are large numbers in both Britain and the USA today. It is these people, no longer immigrants, though frequently described inaccurately as such, who are still disproportionately over-represented in our psychiatric hospitals and institutions.

A powerful explanation for this phenomenon is put forward by Littlewood and Lipsedge in their seminal work *Aliens and Alienists* (1989). They argue that the dominant social group actively alienates those who are perceived as different. As the dominant group, or 'alienists', have no adequate frame of reference for judging the values and behaviours of those from different cultures, they are more likely to describe behaviour they do not understand as deviant or sick. Furthermore, the experience of being discriminated against has the potential to exacerbate the incidence of 'strange' or 'different' behaviour in the 'alien' group, thus increasing the likelihood of receiving a diagnosis of mental illness.

The suggestion that black or Asian ethnic groups may be genetically predisposed towards certain forms of mental illness is one that has been repeatedly made but never proved. Even within genetic science it is difficult to differentiate genes associated with the cause, rather than the symptoms, of specific diseases, and while research has shown 'correlations' between race and some diseases, such correlations may be the result of environmental factors such as diet, living conditions or the experience of prejudice, rather than of genetics (Griffith, 2002). Clearly a genetic basis for mental illness in black people would be a convenient discovery, as the only other explanation for the disproportionate representation of this racial group in the psychiatric statistics would have to include factors such as racial discrimination, social inequality, or lack of understanding (or worse) between (white) doctors and (black) patients. The disturbing and problematic relationship between race, culture and psychiatry is discussed further in Chapter 5.

Psychotherapy and counselling

Historically, psychoanalysis was unavailable to several classes of people, such as those who were thought to be less intelligent or insufficiently verbal or articulate. It has always been inaccessible to those who cannot devote sufficient time to treatment or cannot afford it. Based on those criteria, coloured people have often been judged unsuitable for psychoanalysis and many other psychodynamic approaches. Littlewood (in Kareem and Littlewood, 2000: 6) identifies the psychotherapeutic neglect of minority groups as a particularly British phenomenon. He describes our society as one in which access to mental health resources is determined in part by wealth and education and in part by racial identity. The black community in Britain, being predominantly working class, is thus faced with a double disadvantage in this area (as indeed in other areas).

The emphasis in the field of counselling has always been on the importance of the relationship between counsellor and client, with Carl Rogers' conditions of empathy, genuineness and unconditional positive regard forming the cornerstones of this all-important relationship. The greater part of the counselling literature historically contains no reference to race as an element in this relationship. The presumption is that 'good' counsellors are effective with all their clients if they are able to establish this kind of genuine, empathic and non-judgemental rapport. The recognition of race as an issue deserving special attention has only begun to develop in the last decade or so. However, it is still the case that black and coloured people have less access to counselling and psychotherapy than whites. Blacks and Asians are viewed by many within these professions as more 'physical' and less verbal, manifesting 'somatic' symptoms rather than genuine psychological problems and deemed to be less capable of psychological insight and self-awareness. For this reason they are more likely to be given physical treatments – prescribed powerful anti-depressants and anti-psychotic drugs or subjected to electro-convulsive therapy – than to be referred for counselling or psychotherapy. As d'Ardenne and Mahtani point out, 'the counselling needs of ethnic clients ... are still a very long way from being heard by the majority culture. This, despite the fact that counselling is above all else about active listening' (d'Ardenne and Mahtani, 1989: 10).

As we have seen, racial prejudice is clearly at work in making therapy unavailable to black and coloured people and other ethnic minority groups, but there appears to be something within the very enterprise of the profession itself which works against the interests and needs of these people. Studies have shown that black and coloured clients are more likely to leave counselling and therapy early, and less likely to have favourable outcomes from treatment. Why should this be so? The most convincing explanation seems to be that all models of counselling and psychotherapy are rooted in white western values. The theory and practice of psychotherapy developed in a white western middle-class milieu, so it is hardly surprising that it should contain within it the values and ideals of that social group. Many writers have drawn attention to this (Katz, 1985; Littlewood and Lipsedge, 1989; Palmer and Laungani, 1999; Fernando, 2002). In a recent paper in *Counselling and Psychotherapy Research*, Sue Cornforth emphasizes what she calls 'an inherent tension within the activity of counselling. The profession has a strong ethical commitment to both equity and self-awareness. However, it works within a western, Eurocentric individualistic and economically based paradigm, which mitigates [*sic*] against both' (Cornforth, 2001: 196). The white western bias within psychotherapy and counselling is of course a reflection of the bias that exists within society at large. Inherent in our institutions, the structure of education, health care and access to housing and employment is a socialization process whereby the values, communication patterns, life-styles and family structures of whites, which comprise the dominant group, are upheld as preferable and therefore normative. There is an implicit assumption that this is the world-view to which all people, regardless of their race, culture or ethnic origin, should aspire. This fails to take into account the different (and equally valid) world-views, which are held by peoples from different cultural and racial backgrounds.

Many studies have compared the cultural values of different racial and ethnic groups. Attention has been drawn to factors such as forms of self-expression, temporal focus (past, present or future), relationships between man and nature, social and familial relationships, systems of decision-making, aesthetic preferences, and so forth. What emerges are marked differences between white Anglo-American values and social systems and those of Asians, Africans or any other ethnic group. All of these differences will have an impact on the process of therapy and counselling. It is striking, however, that some of the central tenets of these enterprises are directly opposed to the values held by groups other than the white western cultures. An example of this is individualism. Central to many therapeutic models is an emphasis on the client's self-fulfilment and personal responsibility, combined with a belief that a person can and should take control of his life, overcome his problems, and carve out his own individual path. This notion is central to the western idea of identity, the healthy acquisition of which is seen as an essentially individual process. Individualism also contains within it ideas about personal boundaries, both physical and psychological. Many Eastern cultures, however, are based on communalism or collectivism. Problems are seen as belonging to the group rather than the individual, and are therefore addressed in a communal context. Groups are organized in complex systems and within that system one's identity is ascribed and not achieved. Ideas of personal space (as understood in the west) are lacking – instead, being a useful and integral part of a group is given high value. Group loyalty and cohesion take precedence over ideas about individual personal development.

A similar difficulty exists in the concept of the self. DeVos, Marsella and Hsu (1985) describe how the western tradition focuses on the development of a solid, well-functioning ego. The inner experience of the self should be clearly delineated from external experiences. In Hindu thought the aim is the opposite – to achieve union with the immutable self, which is central to an understanding of the harmony with the totality of the universe. Palmer and Laungani (1999) point to further contrasts in culture in such areas as cognitivism and emotionalism, free will and determinism, materialism and spiritualism. All of these notions are central to the theories underlying psychotherapy and counselling and will have powerful influences on how a client expresses himself, his expectations from the therapist, his assumptions around the origins and causes of his problems, and his ideas about how those difficulties might best be overcome. Triandis (1985) draws attention to the contrast between 'tight' highly regulated cultures and 'loose' heterogeneous cultures, between 'contact' cultures and 'no-contact' cultures, and d'Ardenne and Mahtani (1989) cite the different modes of non-verbal communication which exist in different racial groups and which directly impact on the process of counselling and therapy.

What is clear, therefore, is that a counselling or psychotherapy process which fails to take into account such cultural gulfs will have little chance of success. The theories that underpin psychotherapy and counselling are based on the values and cultural practices of one (white western) culture. They are often upheld, however, as a kind of universal psychological blueprint. To attempt to impose this model on other cultural groups smacks of the arrogance and assumed superiority which has been central to the white man's relationship with other racial groups since time immemorial. We should not be surprised, therefore, that clients from ethnic minorities who do make it to the therapy room, despite the odds, are likely to leave quickly.

Kareem (in Kareem and Littlewood, 2000: 29) cites our understanding of the sense of loss as an example of the difference between western and non-western cultures. Bowlby's theories of attachment and loss and the central part for human development played by the bonding between the human infant and its biological mother are generally accepted by most psychotherapists and counsellors as a kind of universal psychological truth. They are taught in most, if not all, training programmes and form the basis for many other theoretical formulations within the field – much of the literature on bereavement, adoption and fostering, for example, is based on John Bowlby's ideas and on the theories which have been developed from his original formulation. Kareem, however, challenges the normative assumption contained in these theories, one of which is that the loss of a parental figure, particularly the mother who feeds the infant, is of paramount psychological significance. He describes how family patterns in many African and West Indian societies are completely different from the western nuclear family unit. In these societies it is the extended family group, encompassing grandparents, uncles, aunts and cousins that is involved in childcare and child-rearing. In this context separation from, or loss of, the biological mother does not have the psychological significance which it is given in western psychological theory. As Kareem points out, white professionals frequently misunderstand the nature of the loss felt by a client who is separated from his *whole* family, and/or impute spurious psychological damage because the client was brought up by multiple adults rather than a single pair. What has happened here, as in other instances, is the transformation of a western cultural pattern into a universal human psychology.

The issue of misunderstanding within the therapeutic enterprise runs deeper than differences in cultural practices. It taps into the history of racial oppression and the racial inequality still inherent within our society. As Littlewood puts it: 'the provision of "white" therapies for "black" people presenting with problems that result from existing patterns of white–black dominance is problematic, to say the least' (Kareem and Littlewood, 2000: 42). The implications of such a situation are that psychotherapy becomes a means by which political tensions and indignation and distress resulting from social injustice are transformed into the less inconvenient form of 'individual' pathology. This is the charge that has most frequently been levelled at the psychoanalytic and psychodynamic varieties of psychotherapy.

The application of psychoanalytic theory to black groups ignores their social and economic circumstances. In these formulations psychological and emotional difficulties are seen as the result of poor ego functioning, uncontrollable id impulses or maladaptive defence mechanisms, rather than having anything to do with poverty or racial oppression. Psychotherapists who are analytically trained learn to work with the inner world only. Consequently there is resistance to dealing with psychological problems that originate in the outer world. However, most black people would admit that the most traumatic feature in their personal lives is that of being black in a white society. While many clinicians acknowledge that the black client is likely to be socially disadvantaged, they see their therapeutic work to be about exploring the client's response to that, rather than encouraging the client to do anything about it. Thus psychoanalysis and psychotherapy become a process of maintaining the status quo and encouraging people to accept things as they are, however inequitable. A more cynical reading of this situation would be that the white therapist enjoys the fruits of dominant group membership and so has a vested interest in the status quo – one which sees people of colour as deprived, inferior or deviant rather than different. The therapist, therefore, has no interest in creating social change – the client's adaptation to the circumstances would be (for the therapist) the more desirable and comfortable outcome. This may be a rather extreme interpretation. However, what is certainly common is a process whereby the 'pathology' is attributed to the client's culture rather than to the client's individual psychology. In this way behaviour, ways of communicating or values that the therapist cannot understand, or cannot fit into the western psychological template, are all attributed to the other's culture which by definition then becomes not different and equally valid, but deviant and inferior.

In recent years there has been an increasing tendency to recognize race as a factor in counselling and psychotherapy. The UKCP and BACP have both set up divisions whose aim is the implementation of good practice within the area of intercultural and cross-cultural counselling and therapy. Some excellent facilities have been established which are devoted to this work, most notably the Nafsiyat intercultural therapy centre, established in London in 1983. There is also a growing body of literature on the subject. In many ways, however, it is still considered a 'specialist' or marginal area of interest, outside the psychotherapeutic mainstream. Although more training courses now include some input on cross-cultural issues, it is usually lamentably small, and more often than not offered as an optional extra workshop or seminar rather than an integral part of the course. In some respects the pendulum has swung away from the traditional psychoanalytic stance in examining these issues, to a point which is also fraught with potential dangers. Theories have been put forward which draw attention to the deprivation and social oppression of minority ethnic and racial groups; they then assume this to be the direct cause of all psychological and emotional difficulties experienced by people in these groups. In extreme examples these theories create a picture of the black person permanently psychologically damaged by the effects of racial discrimination – an individual incapable of ever developing positive self-esteem or a degree of mental health. The problems with this view are twofold. Firstly it takes no account of the variety of individual responses to the effects of oppression and stress and assumes that all members of visible racial and ethnic groups are socially oppressed and have suffered the consequence of severe psychological damage. Secondly it attributes all the difficulties that a black client might bring to therapy as being related to, or directly caused by, his race.

The notion that race is an issue only for the black client is one that is prevalent in many texts devoted to the subject of race in counselling and therapy. Robert Carter challenges this idea and emphasizes the importance of race as part of everyone's identity. In an overview of the mental health literature he concludes that race as a factor in this field is mentioned only in the context of victims of racism. Whites are 'seldom explicitly included in the discussion of racial effects on individuals and society' (Carter, 1995: 24). He stresses the need for us to take into account the importance of race as an element of experience for white people as well as black and coloured people, a view reiterated by Kareem who believes that the issue of race is rarely absent, even when one shares a client's ethnic and cultural identity. He puts the notion of culture into a wider context when he says, 'beyond the fact of our shared humanity, individuals are unique and distinct from each other and thus there is always an interpersonal and "intercultural" dimension to any encounter between two people, including that between therapist and client' (Kareem and Littlewood, 2000: 19).

The idea of a white racial identity is one that is rarely explored in the psychotherapy literature. There appear to be several reasons for this. Most white westerners associate an emphasis on white identity with racist groups such as the Ku Klux Klan and the BNP. Socially aware or 'politically correct' liberal whites would automatically eschew such an association. By distancing themselves from an identity that is associated with racism, white people are in the position of avoiding or not acknowledging their racial group membership. Nevertheless the fact remains that whites are socialized to feel superior to 'racial/ethnic' people by virtue of their white skin alone. 'This sense of white superiority is so prevalent that it operates as a racial norm in our society, on an individual, institutional, and cultural level' (Carter, 1995: 103). This leaves the white person in an untenable position – feeling superior, but unable to acknowledge it (to self or others) or to act on it. Avoidance of the issue is the most common strategy. Being forced to confront it by the presence of a black or coloured person can induce confusion and anxiety. Such uncomfortable feelings can be all too easily allayed by the notion that race is the other person's issue rather than one's own. Certainly race is seen as an element in experience by black people, but not by white people. Frantz Fanon eloquently writes, 'The white man is sealed in his whiteness. The black man in his blackness' (Fanon, 1986: 11). The difference is that the black man is aware of this, the white man is not. One of the effects of this awareness is internalized racism. Just as white people are socialized to feel that a white skin is superior to a black skin, so are black people. The effects of a deeply embedded sense of inferiority, which may not even be totally within awareness, can be deeply damaging and long-lasting. If a therapist fails to address the issue of race effectively, he can collude in the black/white dominance paradigm and in effect reinforce the internalized racism present in the client's view of himself.

The need for therapists and counsellors to explore and understand their own values and the influence of their own race and culture on those values cannot be understated.

Empathy is not enough – that can be used as the basis of what has been called the 'myth of sameness' (Smith, 1985). If a counsellor is unaware of the assumptions and biases inherent in her own racial and cultural group, she will be unable to relate to a client from a different group without those biases having a detrimental effect on the relationship. Similarly a counsellor who claims to be non-judgemental with all clients, regardless of colour, may well be rationalizing and avoiding difficult inner racial conflicts. Being non-judgemental is a laudable goal, rarely an achievable state.

Racial awareness and identity are part of human development and include the absorption of stereotypes about racial groups at a very early age. Like gender, race-appropriate roles and behaviour are communicated and learned through socialization. For the contemporary white person part of this process is the denial of white identity because of the ensuing discomfort and ambivalence associated with it. Carter (1995) proposes a model of racial identity awareness ranging from low awareness to high awareness, which he applies to both black and white people. In order to understand what is happening in any counselling relationship (black/white, white/black, black/black, white/white) he suggests it is vital to assess each person's level of racial identity awareness.

Contemporary literature and research refutes categorically the notion that black and ethnic minority groups cannot benefit from psychotherapy and counselling because of some inherent lack of self-awareness or psychological insight specific to their racial group (Moorhouse, 2000). Awareness is growing that failure in this field is due to practitioners' inadequacies, or the bias in psychological theory, rather than some deficit in the client. Littlewood points to the experience in the USA where family therapy has been particularly successful with minority racial groups, perhaps because the theory in this model eschews individual developmental notions in favour of an approach derived from a family's shared values understood through systems theory (Kareem and Littlewood, 2000: 10).

When two people from different cultural or ethnic backgrounds meet for counselling or psychotherapy they both bring with them preconceptions about the other. These preconceptions will be heavily informed by both the history of their respective ethnic groups (colonialism, oppression, slavery, and so on) and the relationship that currently exists in our society between white and non-white groups (continuing inequality and racial discrimination). It is the responsibility of the therapist to address these issues in order for there to be any chance of therapeutic effectiveness. All too often therapists avoid such interventions because of their own discomfort and their desire to appear 'liberal' and 'colour blind'. The effect of this is to create in the therapy room a mirror image of the situation in society at large, where the person from the minority group feels devalued, misunderstood, patronized or worse. Almost certainly there would be an unwillingness to disclose feelings and details about personal experiences involving racial identity or racial discrimination with any hope of being truly understood. Psychotherapy should be about the totality of a person's being. As Kareem remarks, 'a psychotherapeutic process that does not take into account the person's whole life experience, or that denies consideration of their race, culture, gender or social values, can only fragment that person' (Kareem and Littlewood, 2000: 16).

It is clear that race and culture are central issues in all counselling and psychotherapeutic relationships. There is a general consciousness in the literature that where there is a racial or cultural difference between therapist and client, the existence of aspects of racism must be assumed. The vast majority of counsellors and therapists in the UK are white and part of the dominant culture. The importance of these professionals examining their own culture and racial issues as well as being familiar with the differences in the values and practices of people from different racial and ethnic groups is recognized as vital. And yet most training courses barely cover such subjects, if at all. Sue, Arendondo and McDivis (1992) suggest that inadequate training is the major reason for therapeutic ineffectiveness in this area. As we have seen, one of the reasons for this lies in the theory which forms the core of counselling and psychotherapy training programmes. Most theoretical models and orientations have not considered the psychological meaning and importance of race and culture; furthermore, many of their central theoretical tenets are founded in normative Eurocentric cultural values.

More disturbing is the idea that racism is embedded in all our social institutions as well as in the socialization and education received by all members of our society. Consequently, those people who train to be counsellors and therapists and those trainers who train them will also have absorbed racist notions which will then be perpetuated in the training and practice of counselling and psychotherapy itself.

3 | Gender

I T IS GENERALLY RECOGNIZED that the relations between men and women throughout history are characterized by the domination of the latter by the former. At the turn of the twenty-first century this state of affairs is beginning to be challenged. Some commentators talk about 'post-feminism' as though the aims of the feminist movement had been achieved, or as though questioning whether they even needed redressing. It is undeniable that social, political and domestic arrangements have changed dramatically in the last fifty years, and that the position of women has improved immeasurably in all areas of life. One of the themes of modern social concern is the disaffection and under-achievement of young men and boys and their decreasing academic performance in comparison with young women and girls. Despite this, the gender balance in work and opportunity in all spheres in the western world is still weighted in favour of men.

In examining the subject of gender, therefore, I intend to look first at the history of men and women in terms of their relative social, political and economic positions. An intrinsic part of this is an examination of feminism, both as a historical and political movement and as an ideology. I then intend to examine the concept of gender, in particular in the context of the psychological, medical and scientific theories that have been brought to bear on it. Finally I aim to analyse the impact of gender within the field of counselling and psychotherapy; in the training and practice of counsellors and therapists and in their relationships with their clients.

Gender relations – a historical overview

The social and economic relationship between men and women has varied considerably over time, and between different societies and cultures. The overwhelming evidence, however, would seem to point to the fact that in most societies, in most places, women have been subordinated to men to a greater or lesser extent.

Early history

Attempts have been made, principally by feminists, to prove the existence of prehistoric matriarchal societies. There appears to be some evidence of societies in which women were held in high esteem in the Neolithic and Bronze Ages, with suggestions of goddess worship derived from archaeological artefacts. Theories abound about the worship of the 'Great Mother Goddess' as central to prehistoric cultures in Europe, Asia and Africa (Miles, 1993). To view such societies as matriarchal is controversial. They were at best egalitarian. In Gerda Lerner's view, if we define matriarchy as a mirror image of patriarchy, no true matriarchal society has ever existed (Lerner, 1986: 31). There appears, however, to be a consensus about the true nature of hunter/gatherer societies. The stereotypical image of man-the-hunter whose greater physical strength provided both the food and the protection for the weak and vulnerable female has been disproved by anthropological evidence. It is now understood that the main food supply in such societies was provided by the women and children – by gathering activities and small-game hunting. Big-game hunting, done by the man, was an infrequent and auxiliary pursuit, and by no means a reliable source of regular food. The gender relations in these societies appear to have been essentially complementary; there was a division of labour by gender, but such divisions carried with them no connotations of superiority or inferiority.

The classical period, however, presents a picture where male supremacy was the norm. In Greece, women were viewed as inferior to men in all respects and had considerable restrictions put on their freedom of movement. Their social role was restricted to the home: domestic management, childbearing and child-rearing. In ancient Rome, too, the patriarchal system held sway – the man was the head of the family and had the power of life and death over all members of his family. Women had no legal status or property rights. Similarly in the western world, as societies became organized and complex, ownership and property evolved as predominantly male rights.

A significant factor in gender relations worldwide is the part played by religion. Rosalind Miles (1993) draws attention to the fact that all the world's major religions are monotheistic, centred round a male god and with beliefs which condemn women to the status of second-class citizens. She sees the emergence of the world's major religions as the foundation of patriarchy; monotheism being built on the idea of men and women as complementary opposites, with men arrogating to themselves all the strengths and virtues, thus relegating women by definition to inferior status. Certainly within Christianity many biblical texts can be cited to support this idea. The story of Adam and Eve gives us woman as created second, from man, to be his companion; on top of this Eve is also the temptress, the one responsible for man's fall from grace. As such there is every justification for her punishment and oppression. In the third century AD St Ambrose is reputed to have said, 'Adam was led to sin by Eve and not Eve by Adam. It is just and right that women accept as lord and master him whom she led to sin' (Ussher, 1991: 44).

In the early years of the medieval period the part that women played, in society and in organized religion, was more significant than in the latter years of this period. Pastoral and agricultural communities tended to be more egalitarian than the more sophisticated and organized urban societies which had emerged by the 1500s. However, women were consistently restricted from land and property ownership as these were dependent on the provision of military service. Within the developing institutions of society – the church, law and administration – women were either totally excluded or held subordinate positions. As societies evolved, the view that women were intellectually inferior meant that the majority of women had no access to education. The growth of urban communities initially gave some women a degree of freedom, as many women ran their own businesses in early medieval times. However, as trade and commerce became increasingly capitalized in the seventeenth century and beyond, women were excluded from ownership and control in this sphere too. Throughout Europe in the pre-industrial period, society consisted of a system of rigid stratification based on birth and wealth. Women took their social status first from their fathers and then from their husbands. In the aristocracy in particular women led very restricted lives, confined mostly to the domestic sphere. For such women the only alternative to marriage which offered a degree of independence and education was enrolment into a religious order. However, the dissolution of the nunneries in the mid-sixteenth century removed that option too. At around the same time there was an increase in literacy and the growth of universities and grammar schools – both of which were exclusively male preserves.

With the Reformation education became marginally more available to women, but at the same time the importance of the institution of marriage came to be firmly established as the basis of social and gender organization. Wives were legally subordinate to their husbands as well as financially dependent on them. Except in some of the lower social classes, inheritance of property and money was strictly through the male line. Women who did have assets were not free to dispose of them, and on marriage such assets became the property of the husband. Divorce was very rare, as it was only available by Act of Parliament, so marriage was for life. Further illustration of the double standards in operation is the fact that in 1650 the death penalty was instituted for female adultery. Men who committed the same act were only guilty of fornication, which carried a lesser penalty. This discrepancy is a stark reflection of the view of women's sexuality as only acceptable in terms of procreation and the maternal instinct. Men's sexuality, however, was seen as an irresistible natural force. Such notions have persisted until recent times.

Europe in the eighteenth and nineteenth centuries
Until the Industrial Revolution in the latter part of the eighteenth century work was organized within the home or within small communities, with men and women often working together for their common good. With the shift to an industrial economy women lost the flexibility they had previously possessed when work had been home-based. They were paid less in the factories than their male counterparts, as well as retaining the responsibility for running the home. The machine age split society into the public and private spheres: the worlds of office and factory versus that of the home. In this new order women were 'granted the privilege of low-grade, exploited occupations, the double burden of waged and domestic labour, and the sole responsibility for child care that has weighed them down ever since' (Miles, 1993: 187). In the higher social classes work was seen solely as the prerogative of men; women were relegated to an exclusively domestic and maternal role.

The nineteenth century was probably the period where patriarchy and the stereotypes associated with it reached their zenith. Men began to define themselves increasingly by their work as their involvement with child-rearing and domestic production declined. Women were viewed as destined by their biological functions to be wives and mothers. The medical model at the time held that the body had a finite supply of energy. Female bodily functions – menstruation, pregnancy, childbirth – were deemed to consume an inordinate amount of this energy, thus rendering women unfit for any mental or intellectual activity. Men were strong; women were delicate and potentially unstable. This was viewed as the natural order. The development of science led to a plethora of theories proposed to support this view: women's brains were smaller than men's, or less evolved; women were more prone to a variety of illnesses which threatened their health and sanity and made them ill-suited to make rational or moral decisions. Such theories were a justification for depriving them of civil and legal rights. The masculine stereotype was seen as the physical and psychological norm; women were an inferior version of this norm.

Many writers have documented the physical and mental indignities to which women have been subjected over the ages. The list is endless: chastity belts in the Middle Ages, menstrual taboos, enforced marriage, female infanticide, suttee in India, footbinding in China, female circumcision and genital mutilation, rape, sexual violence and sexual objectification through pornography. Many if not all of these practices focus on women's sexuality and its control by men. This element of the relationship between men and women has always been a source of tension and a point at which the nature of that relationship – mutuality or domination/submission – is thrown into sharp relief. It is intimately connected with views about the nature of sexuality *per se*, the biological function of reproduction, and the social role and rights of women. In the western world in the latter part of the twentieth century sexual freedom became a central part of women's demands for equality. In the nineteenth century sex was still taboo as a subject for open debate. Initially, therefore, women's struggles for greater freedom focused exclusively on political and civil rights.

The beginnings of emancipation

The women's rights movement began to develop in the mid-nineteenth century in the USA with the Seneca Falls Convention of 1848 and the resulting Declaration of Sentiments in which women claimed the liberty and equality expounded in the American Declaration of Independence. This led to the founding of women's suffrage movements in both the USA and Britain. There had been demands before this time by women for an amelioration in their position, both in France following the French Revolution, where the newly-won rights were restricted to men, and in England with the publication in 1792 of *A Vindication of the Rights of Women* by Mary Wollstonecraft. However, it was not until the late nineteenth and early twentieth centuries that the demand for equal rights for women really took hold and gained sufficient momentum to produce results. The suffrage movement in the UK united women from all social classes, with energies focused initially on the issue of political representation. With the granting of the vote (for women over thirty in 1918 and those under thirty in 1928) there followed swiftly a number of changes in the law which considerably improved women's social and legal positions – for example allowing women access to public office, granting them greater property rights and parity with men in such issues as divorce, and a decrease in the gender differential in pay. The social changes brought about by two world wars led to a considerable shift in the relative positions of men and women. The issue of equal rights for women became a matter for public debate, and has remained so ever since.

The suffrage movement is often described as the 'first wave' of feminism, the 'second wave' occurring in the 1960s and 1970s. But feminist thought and action continued throughout the twentieth century. Sheila Rowbotham (1999) identifies the 1950s as a time which was particularly problematic in women's demands for greater social equality. The post-war period saw many women, who had done responsible and fulfilling jobs during the war, revert to the role of housewife as men were demobilized and returned to the workforce. But the war experience left many women ultimately dissatisfied with the roles they had filled before. The demand for social change was gaining momentum. Further difficulties, however, were created by the post-war emphasis on the family as the building block of a stable society. Within the stereotypical family the man went out to work and the woman stayed at home. Such a stereotype was reinforced by the psychological thought at the time which placed great emphasis on the centrality of the mother–child relationship. The theories of D.W. Winnicott and John Bowlby roused fears that maternal deprivation was psychologically damaging for babies and young children. This had the effect of undermining women's demands for nurseries and after-school care. The centrality of the family, and the traditional female role within it, still made it difficult for women to gain equal access to education and employment. Many would claim that this continues to be the case in the present day.

The 1960s saw the beginning of another period of social ferment and upheaval. Opportunities for women were back on the political agenda. Abortion was legalized and, with the advent of the contraceptive pill, birth control became widely available. Further reforms to matrimonial and divorce laws gave women greater financial independence. The Women's Liberation Movement in the 1970s focused on women's rights in the areas of family, sexuality and work. In this decade the Sex Discrimination Act and the Equal Pay Act came into force, and the Equal Opportunities Commission was set up. The social changes in the latter part of the twentieth century were extensive. Sexual freedom and permissiveness led to the social acceptance of divorce, single mothers, and couples living together and having children without getting married. Nearly all areas of work have now been opened to women. Women have achieved positions as business leaders, cabinet ministers, high court judges, consultant surgeons and even (in 1994) Church of England priests. But, despite this, their representation in such positions of power is still lamentably small, and top women are still paid less than top men.

The feminist debate

Central to the feminist ideology that emerged in the 1960s and 1970s is the equality–difference debate – one that still rages, as its significance has implications for women and men today no less than it did fifty years ago. Put starkly, the debate is over whether women should struggle to be equal to men, or whether they should demand reforms based on their differences from men. Since feminist thought and action have always attacked the male assumption of superiority, they led many into the position of challenging the assumption of natural differences *per se*. This was an understandable position given that historically women have always been accorded inferior status precisely because of assumed natural sex differences. Any admission that there were such differences appeared to be supporting the ideology that underpinned patriarchal exclusion. Extreme feminists have seen all men as oppressors and heterosexuality as an instrument of male oppression. Thus lesbianism becomes a political choice and the only way to achieve true female liberation.

Other feminists have argued for an acceptance of the differences between men and women together with a recognition that these differences carry with them no connotations of superiority or inferiority. 'Female' qualities should be seen as equally important and valuable as 'male' ones, or maybe even more so. The problem inherent in this argument is that it seems impossible to argue for difference without creating some kind of hierarchy. As with so many of the debates around discrimination where, historically, oppression has been justified by biological differences, there is a difficulty in suggesting the recognition of such differences as part of the fight against discriminatory treatment. Such a suggestion can revive the spectre of sexist domination of women by men. Controversy is also generated by the question of what kinds of differences are to be recognized – biological? psychological? physical? How and by whom are these differences to be defined?

This debate dovetails with the other central theme of feminist ideology and women's struggles for improvements in their social position – the insoluble dilemma of the demands of motherhood and work. Some would argue that reproduction is a burden, and a cause of women's oppression. Others see motherhood as one of the great pleasures of being a woman, but feel that the biology of reproduction should not disadvantage women who also want a career. The availability of reliable contraception has given women greater choice over when, or whether, to have children. There have, however, been few social advances to help those women who choose to have both career and family, and the experience of most in this position is that even short career breaks for pregnancy and childbirth have detrimental effects on a woman's career path. Furthermore, in a family where both partners work, the burden of domestic and childcare arrangements still falls principally on the woman.

Contemporary gender relations in the UK
The current state of legislation in Britain should theoretically grant equality of opportunity to men and women in all spheres of work and public life. The picture portrayed by actual achievement is rather different. Twenty years ago,

for the first time, girls gained parity with boys in terms of success at school examinations. By 2001 girls were achieving significantly better results both at school and at the level of higher education. This reversal of past trends has not yet been carried through to the workplace. Sixty-seven per cent of managers and administrators are still men, while 71 per cent of clerical and secretarial staff are women. The earnings of female employees working full time are on average 82 per cent those of male full-time employees, with women being highly represented in the part-time workforce which is, almost by definition, less well paid. Only 18 per cent of Members of Parliament and 8 per cent of High Court judges are women (EOC, 2001). Even allowing for the time it takes for trends to adjust to the entry of qualified women to the workforce, fewer women occupy high-status positions than would be expected from their numbers in the workforce as a whole. This is the case even in occupations where women are in a numerical majority, for example counselling, of which more later. Even when women do make it to the top, their financial rewards are significantly less than men. A survey in the *Independent* in 1999 revealed that male academics in almost every university and college in the UK were being paid more than women – in some instances the average salary differential was as much as £20,000 per year (Clare, 2000: 94).

It is generally accepted (and deplored by some) that gender stereotyping plays a large part in the kind of work chosen by, or made available to, men and women. There is 'men's work' and 'women's work'. Such ideas can have a big impact both on levels of aspiration and educational and professional opportunities. Although gender stereotypes tend to reflect traditional ideas about what men and women are good at, studies have shown that what has a bigger impact is the fact that work carried out by men, whatever it is, has a higher status. Thus jobs that shift from being predominantly performed by men to becoming women's occupations lose social status (Archer and Lloyd, 1985: 239) – an indication of the extent to which the differential in gender status is embedded in our social attitudes.

Whereas the world of employment presents a picture where women still receive a raw deal, the social picture is rather different. The decline of the traditional family unit and the increase in the number of households headed by single females is depriving men of involvement in family life and parenting to an extent which is causing considerable concern. The male role in the nineteenth century and the beginning of the twentieth century was characterized as that of the breadwinner. As women's earning power rises, and, more significantly, women embrace a willingness to live lives independent of men, the position of man is severely weakened. He becomes, at best, the provider of sperm, after which he serves no useful purpose. The development of reproductive technology such as AID carries this to its logical conclusion, dispensing with the need for men as an actual presence in the lives of women and their children. As Anthony Clare puts it, 'artificial insemination by anonymous donor strikes directly at masculinity and fatherhood' (Clare, 2001: 107). Clare's analysis in *On Men – Masculinity in Crisis* is that men have only themselves to blame for their precarious position. Their social estrangement is caused by their own unwillingness to relinquish the outmoded stereotype of masculinity – the stereotype in which maleness resides in such values as 'control, indifference to feelings and a ruthless pursuit of power' which produce what he calls 'a psychopathic masculinity' (ibid.: 217).

The tension between men and women has always existed and continues to do so. The debate still rages around their respective roles, rights and positions in society. Such a debate encompasses ideas about the differences and similarities between the genders – their characteristics, attributes and how these can best be utilized for both individual satisfaction and social harmony. It is to these ideas that I shall now turn.

Gender and gender identity – some of the theories

Biology versus environment

The use of the words 'sex', 'gender', 'sexual identity' and 'gender identity' can be confusing. To some extent the confusion over the meanings of these words and terms reflects the unresolved issues surrounding this whole topic. My understanding and my use of these terms are as follows. 'Sex' refers to a biological (usually anatomical and/or genetic) classification as belonging to either the group of males or the group of females. 'Gender' refers to an individual's own felt sense of identity as belonging to either the group of males or the group of females. 'Sexual identity' refers to an individual's felt sense of belonging to a group of people whose sexual practices are characterized as heterosexual, homosexual, bisexual, and so on. This is discussed fully in the next chapter. The debate central to the issue of gender and gender identity is the origin of the observed differences in behaviour between men and women, boys and girls. Do these differences stem from innate biological distinctions, or are they socially learned, the result of environmental influences? Some would say that our identity as belonging to a particular gender is entirely socially constructed. Others would claim that gender differences are deeply rooted in biology. It's the old nature/nurture argument writ large!

Observation, and statistics, tell us that there are differences between male and female behaviour that are significant enough to be categorized in generalizations such as the following: men appear to be more aggressive, competitive, physical, mathematically gifted than women. Women appear to be more emotional, nurturing, verbally adept than men. But why should this be so? Clearly if these differences are biologically determined there is little that can be done to change things, should we wish to do so, short of tinkering with our hormones or our genes – options which of course are becoming more viable with current scientific advances. If, however, these differences are the product of social conditioning, we have the power to reorganize things differently.

It is no accident that the history of the theories that have gained ascendance in this field mirrors the history of the social relations between men and women. Until second-wave feminism, the view that women were 'naturally' inferior to men was largely unchallenged. This hierarchy was seen for a long time as ordained by God, or by some grand cosmological order. The advances in science and anatomy in the eighteenth century led to greater understanding of the physical differences between men and women and the workings of the reproductive organs. This was the beginning of biological determinism – male/female physical differences being seen as the cause of the male/female distinction itself (Nicholson, 1998: 195). In the 1960s, originating with Robert Stoller's work *Sex and Gender* (1968), the theory of gender as socially constructed began to gain credence. It was immensely popular with feminist activists as it focused on social processes and structures – the very things they wanted to change. According to the conditioning view, gender differences in temperament and ability are to be understood not in terms of female inadequacy and weakness; rather, they are the result of societal (male) pressures that have resulted in female subservience and under-achievement.

The response to this notion has been a resurgence in the view that male/female differences are biological – not only that, but that they are rooted in their evolutionary origins. The 1980s and 1990s saw a renewed interest in social Darwinism with E.O. Wilson's sociobiology and Stevens and Price's evolutionary psychiatry. These theorists claim that behaviours such as aggression and maternalism are encoded in the genes. If we believe that the roles of men and women reflect their evolutionary origins, the natural place for women is in the home, looking after children. It follows that drastic social changes would be both undesirable and doomed to failure. It would seem no accident that these theories have emerged – or reappeared – at the very time when the traditional position of men within the social structure is under threat.

The biological determinists assert that there are innate physical and psychological differences between men and women and that these differences centre on the division of labour whereby women take responsibility for child-rearing and men take responsibility for hunting and warfare. This division is seen as biologically rather than socially determined (Stevens and Price, 1996: 163), although the implications seem to be that the reason for the evolution of these differences lay originally in the demands of the environment and the needs involved in species survival. This theory is based on a conceptualization of the hunter/gatherer societies which we now know to be fallacious, and also takes no account of the effects of evolution since that time. We are no longer living in caves, fighting off predators. If, as the theory of evolutionary adaptation implies, we change according to the different circumstances in which we find ourselves, then the adaptations appropriate to the Stone Age would have been overtaken by now.

Another biological theory holds that our gender identity is determined by our hormones. The critical factor here is the extent to which the brain of a foetus is exposed to male hormones prior to birth. Given that all human foetuses start as biologically female, there is a point in development when the Y chromosome in the genetically male foetus stimulates the production of male hormones that cause the sexual differentiation of the brain. In their convincingly argued book, *Brain Sex* (1989), Moir and Jessel make out the case for this being the basis for all the observed differences in behaviour, attitudes and feelings between men and women. For other writers in the field these theories are held to be too simplistic. Arguments have been put forward suggesting that the differences discovered in the brains of men and women are the result of the social environment of an individual during development rather than genetic or hormonal influences (Rose, Lewontin and Kamin, 1984: 142). The argument that the existence of a physical difference in a physical organ is automatically proof of a physical cause has been seriously questioned. Our understanding of the relationship between mind and body now recognizes the complexity of this relationship and the multiplicity of potential influences. Traumatic events, emotional responses and physical and psychological environmental factors all have an impact on the brain's development and functioning, as well as any biological or genetic distinctions present at birth.

The theories of the biological determinists are seen by many as dangerous because they appear to recommend a continuation of the status quo, and take no account of the social pressures and expectations which stem from gender stereotypes. That such stereotypes persist is undeniable. Despite the social changes that have taken place since the middle of the twentieth century, there is still an expectation for boys to be more aggressive, physical, mechanically minded and so on, and for girls to be nurturing, emotional and dependent. Over and above this, the qualities that we categorize as being typically 'masculine' carry more positive connotations than the qualities we categorize as being typically 'feminine' (Archer and Lloyd, 1985: 40). 'Male' attributes include qualities such as courage, confidence, ambition, stability; females are associated with characteristics such as dependence, passivity, frivolity, weakness and sentimentality. It has been observed that parents respond differently to their baby boys than to their baby girls

(Rose et al., 1984: 142), interacting in a more robust manner with boys and in a more caring and gentle way with girls. This would seem to confirm social conditioning theory. And yet it could also be argued that it is something in the baby, himself or herself, that stimulates such different parental responses.

There are many characteristics and attributes cited as differentiating men from women. Studies purport to show that, among other things, men are better at mathematics, activities involving 'spatial ability', have better hand–eye coordination than women, and that women are more fluent at languages, have greater sensitivity to sound, smell and pain and have better memories than men (Moir and Jessel, 1989; Stevens and Price, 1996). Some writers have attempted to either disprove or minimize the significance of such studies, claiming that the tests were unscientific, unsound or that the differences that result are so minimal as to be negligible (Rose et al., 1984; Archer and Lloyd, 1985; Clare, 2001). There is, however, one feature associated with each gender that is overwhelmingly supported by both observation and statistics: male aggression and female depression. The populations of our prisons and our mental hospitals seem to show that *in extremis* men commit violent crimes and women succumb to depression and mental illness. Depending on which camp you belong to, this can be explained either by biology (men are naturally aggressive, women are naturally more emotional and inward-looking) or by conditioning (men and women both respond to social expectations which demand certain behaviours of them and inhibit others). Feminists would go further in respect of female depression and explain it as the inevitable consequence of male oppression. Clare makes out a convincing case for the effects of cultural and societal pressures on the incidence of male violence citing, among other arguments, the significantly higher rates of male violence in countries where the masculine code of 'machismo' is strongest. In his view, 'maleness and aggression do not have to go together' (Clare, 2000: 59); one of the reasons why they have come to be so closely associated is the fact that in our modern capitalist society men are defined by actions and what they do rather than by who they are – their 'being'.

It would seem nonsensical, therefore, to deny that there are real and distinct differences between men and women. The difficulty arises when those differences are evaluated. The traditional outcome of such an evaluation is to view the differences as necessarily involving female deficiencies. It is this view which sparked the feminist movement and has fuelled much of the writing attempting to prove that *all* gender differences are environmentally caused. Steven Pinker (2002) cogently argues the case that gender differences are indeed rooted in biology, but that those differences do not have to imply either inferiority or superiority. We seem now to have arrived at a point where we need to accept and value both those qualities that we associate with men and those qualities that we associate with women. At the same time we need to be aware of the dangers inherent in the stereotypical male and female qualities. As Gerda Lerner puts it:

> Regardless of whether such qualities as aggressiveness or nurturance are genetically or culturally transmitted it should be obvious that the aggressiveness of males, which may have been highly functional in the Stone Age, is threatening human survival in the nuclear age. At a time when over-population and exhaustion of natural resources represent a real danger for human survival, to curb women's procreative capacities may be more 'adaptive' than to foster them. (Lerner, 1986: 20)

Psychological theories

Classical psychoanalytic theory has played a large part in the development of theories surrounding gender and gender identity. Freud believed that both maleness and femaleness are present in all human beings and that this innate bisexuality has consequences for both normal and abnormal development (Freud, 1905). However, he also believed that maleness and masculinity are the primary and more natural states and that both men and women consider femaleness and femininity less valuable (Freud, 1933). Freud's theory of psychosexual development centres around the male child whose chances of successfully negotiating the various stages of the oedipal complex are considerably greater than the female child. The main reason for this is the anatomical fact of the male penis. Resolution of the oedipal conflict rests on observation (in both sexes) of the female deficiency in this department. For the boy, the resulting castration anxiety leads to his renouncing his oedipal desires for his mother and completes this phase of his development. For the girl, there is a less clear-cut impetus for oedipal resolution as she is already castrated, so to speak. This, for Freud, signified a seriously compromised super-ego. As a result, women, he believed, have less judgement and sense of justice than men, and are more prone to jealousy and narcissism – these being the by-products of penis envy.

The phallocentric nature of Freud's theory, based as it was on an assumption of the natural superiority of the male genital organs, has aroused criticism from its inception to the present day. Karen Horney (1924) was one of the first to challenge Freud's notion of penis envy, suggesting that issues of power and control and the influence of the male position in society played a part in the formulations put forward by Freud and other male psychoanalysts. More recently Anthony Clare's analysis of Freud's concept of penis envy concludes that it is a classic example of projection – the projection of male anxiety about the actual basis of phallic superiority and male potency onto women in the form of spurious female desire for a penis (Clare, 2000: 196).

Not surprisingly, psychoanalytic theory about female psychology has proved to be fiercely controversial among feminists from the 1920s to the present. Early psychoanalytic theory stressed the primacy of the father in human development as well as centring psychosexual issues on the male child and the male appendage. By the 1970s psychoanalysis had gained a reputation as an ideology which encouraged women to adapt to the situations which created not only their unhappiness, but also their depression and psychological problems. However, many post-Freudians had emphasized the importance of the maternal role (for example, Winnicott and Bowlby) and with second-wave feminism came a reassessment of the value of psychoanalytic thought to an understanding of female psychology. Orbach and Eichenbaum (1984; 1985) stressed the importance of the mother/daughter relationship and in so doing reassessed the nature of men's and women's dependency. They suggest that women are brought up to meet men's dependency needs, not their own. Consequently women have difficulty achieving autonomy and independence as they have permanently unsatisfied dependency needs which hold them back. Men, meanwhile, are well catered for by their mothers and wives and are therefore in a better position to separate and individuate. Moreover, in order for a man to provide nurture to a woman he has to draw on his own 'femininity' – that aspect of himself which he feels he has to repress in order to be a man. To provide what a woman needs, therefore, a man is involved in a process that directly threatens his concept of his self.

This conflict is seen by many theorists as the central element of male psychology – the need to separate from women, combined with the fear of loss of identity and 'maleness' when intimacy with a woman is achieved (Lemma-Wright, 1995: 47). This is the explanation given for men's difficulty in sustaining intimacy and for a purported male fear of women and female sexuality. The history of women's oppression can be told in terms of male attempts to cover, hide, control and contain women's bodies and physicality. Parallel to this, women have throughout history been seen as of use *only* for their bodies – for the pleasure of man and to give birth to his children. This is seen as a classic conflict between desire and fear – which results in portraying women as sinister, destructive and insatiable. They are witches, whores and madonnas all at the same time. A woman can arouse a man's desires, and in so doing she triggers his fear of losing his male identity, a fear of being engulfed and no longer separate, and for that reason she is an object to be feared and if possible kept under control.

Gender in counselling and psychotherapy

Of all the issues under consideration in this book, that of women as the oppressed 'minority' has a particular feature in that within the field of psychotherapy and counselling women are in the majority, both as practitioners and clients. Numerically, the majority of counsellors and thera- pists embody the characteristics of the dominant or 'nor- mative' group in respect of the colour of their skin (white), their sexual orientation (heterosexual), and in their physi- cal and mental health (able-bodied, and not suffering from a diagnosed mental illness). However, the majority of counsellors, therapists and clients come from what is tradi- tionally perceived to be the oppressed group when it comes to gender – most of them are women (Coldridge and Mickelborough, 2003). Feminists would argue that, as far as female clients are concerned, this is precisely because they have been oppressed and therefore deserve special attention within the field of psychological thought. As we have seen, traditional psychoanalytic theory – and indeed the theory within all schools of psychotherapy – has been formulated predominantly by men. The earliest theories of human development focused specifically on the develop- ment of the male infant and, feminists would argue, perpe- trated the notion of male superiority and importance. This has been very largely redressed by later theorists and in particular by the feminist movement of the 1970s and beyond. Indeed there exists an impressive body of literature devoted to the subject of feminine psychology and feminist counselling and psychotherapy.

The fact remains, however, that men are in the minority in the field of counselling and psychotherapy, both as trainees, practitioners and clients. Why should this be so? And given that it is the case, what are the implications for the experiences of men who come to this field, either as would-be practitioners, practitioners or clients?

Why more female clients?

Gender stereotypes contain the idea that women are more comfortable with their feelings than men. This would clearly make them both more drawn to the 'talking therapies' and more suitable, and even successful, as clients of such. My own belief is that there is no innate gender difference between the capacity of men and women to identify, talk about and make sense of their own emotions, or those of others, but that cultural and environmental influences play a big part in encouraging some men (and boys) not to develop this capacity. There is instead heavy emphasis on the need for men to channel their energies into action, achievement and goal-oriented activities. Men are encouraged to adopt the attitude that they should be strong and sort out their own problems. Seeking help is seen as an indication that alone you are unable to do this. This is viewed as a weakness – and an admission of failure to meet the 'male' standard of behaviour. Women, on the other hand, are more likely to accept that vulnerability is part of being human (or female?) and that both asking for help and talking about their problems is an acceptable way of dealing with the inevitable difficulties of life.

A more radical explanation for the preponderance of female clients is that the oppression they experience at the hands of men makes them ill, renders them susceptible to depression, or even sends them mad. It has been suggested that women's lack of status in society is experienced as a loss which generates frustration and anger. These emotions can find no expression precisely because of women's power-less social position – they therefore turn inward, which may result in depression (Chesler, 1972). Gender-role socializa-tion has been compared to the psychological condition of 'learned helplessness' which characterizes depression in terms of passivity, lack of observable aggression and reduced effectiveness in solving problems (Litman, 1978). At its most extreme this line of reasoning would claim that women's distress is the result of institutional and individual oppression, not individual pathology. Misogyny either causes female madness or labels women as mad in order to silence them (Ussher, 1991). The general tenet of this school of thought is that sexism has adverse effects on women's emotional and psychological health – this is why they present for psychological help in greater numbers than men. This view forms the basis for much of the literature on feminist counselling and psychotherapy, which seeks to redress this situation by encouraging women to develop greater self-confidence and autonomy; to challenge patri-archy and thus free themselves from the psychological ill-health that it creates.

Attention is beginning to be drawn to the gender imbal-ance in clients of counselling and psychotherapy (Garde, 2003; Wheeler, 2003). Despite the fact that men, generally speaking, are less healthy than women, and are more likely to commit suicide than women, they are less likely to seek psychological help than women at a ratio of about 2:1 (Millar, 2003). What appears to underlie this are deep-seated cultural stereotypes about what constitutes mas-culinity which inhibit men from utilizing resources such as counselling or therapy.

Why more female counsellors and therapists?
The same arguments about gender stereotyping would apply here. Given that women are, generally speaking, more comfortable expressing their feelings and talking about their problems than men, it follows that they are going to be better at facilitating others to do the same. There is also a high incidence of people drawn to train as counsellors and therapists by having been through personal difficulties of their own, and having been helped by therapeutic experiences. The over-representation of women as clients of therapy would therefore carry through to their preponderance as practitioners. Similarly, all training programmes require of their participants an extensive period of personal therapy, usually concurrent with the training itself. As a factor within the training for the profession this is more likely to appeal to prospective female applicants than to their male counterparts.

The ethos, modes of communication and forms of expression which pertain in counselling and psychotherapy training courses are all those which are likely to be more congenial and familiar to women than to men. There is a culture of personal disclosure, empathic expression and sharing of emotions and experiences which many men experience as both unfamiliar and excluding (Gillon, 2002). The qualities and skills that trainee counsellors are required to demonstrate are undeniably those that are traditionally viewed as being 'female' attributes: empathy, understanding, self-awareness, intuition and sensitivity.

A more practical reason for women being attracted to work as counsellors and therapists is the potential flexibility that such work offers. There is considerable scope for organizing working hours round such commitments as childcare and domestic management. Many female counsellors work part-time for this reason, their earnings being 'supplementary' to the household income. By the same token it is relatively hard to make a full-time or financially viable career out of working as a counsellor or psychotherapist. There are very few full-time psychotherapy posts within the National Health Service and competition within the private sector is fierce. It is not surprising, therefore, that in a profession populated predominantly by women, men are heavily over-represented in the full-time posts, in the management of training facilities and counselling centres and in the top academic posts in universities.

Men as counsellors and clients
The experience of many men who undertake training to be counsellors and psychotherapists is that they are discounted, victimized or at the very least overlooked as trainees. In any training I have been a part of, either as participant or trainer, men have been both a significant minority and more likely to fail to complete the course than their female colleagues. I have observed that, as clients, men attract more hostility and criticism in (all-female) supervision groups than female clients. In psychoanalytic terms this could be explained as the individual male client, trainee or therapist being the recipient of the projections of their female colleagues and therapists – becoming the focus of the repressed aggression resulting from years of oppression by a male-dominated society. It could also be understood in terms of role reversal. In society at large women are the disadvantaged 'minority' group, fighting to achieve equal standing with men. Finding themselves in an environment where they are, for once, in the majority, their behaviour towards the hapless men who happen to stray into that world has the potential to contain within it elements of revenge.

Another significant factor which militates against men in the field of counselling and therapy, either as practitioners or clients, is the growing public perception of all men as potential abusers (Clare, 2000: 185). The high incidence of male violence generally, combined with an increasing awareness of the problems of child abuse and domestic violence, has had the effect of painting a picture of men as beings who can barely contain their impulses to rape and assault women and children at every available opportunity. Cases of assault (sexual or otherwise) on female clients by their male therapists receive much publicity and add fuel to this concern. Similarly, the furore created by the False Memory/Repressed Memory Syndrome debate has further blackened the case for men. When Bass and Davis published their book *The Courage to Heal* in 1988, there was a sudden and huge increase in young women accusing their fathers of incest when they were children, both in the US and in Britain. Dealing with this trauma is not appropriate work for male therapists who by virtue of their gender alone are highly suspect. Many male counsellors and therapists in private practice feel the need to instigate elaborate measures in order to convey to their female clients the absence of their desire to abuse or exploit them.

Gender in the therapeutic relationship
It is surprising to discover that in all the literature about the counselling and psychotherapeutic relationship, there is almost nothing on the subject of the impact of gender. Given the history of the social relationship between men and women and the existing tensions within their respective current positions, it would seem inevitable that in any therapeutic dyad the gender of client and therapist would play a part in their relationship.

There is, as mentioned, a huge body of literature on the subject of feminist counselling. The philosophy underlying most of this is that women's psychology and experiences are specific and different from men's – at least partly due to the effects of patriarchy and the historical oppression of women. The conclusion that is drawn is that women need a particular type of counselling to help them escape from their stereotypical roles and overcome their socialized passivity and depression. This involves developing women's self-esteem and self-confidence and facilitating them in greater assertiveness (Chaplin, 1988; McLeod, 1994; Lawrence and Maguire, 1997). It is axiomatic that feminist therapy is carried out by women, for women.

In her chapter entitled 'Counselling and Gender' in the *Handbook of Counselling in Britain* (1989), Jocelyn Chaplin provides a brief but succinct outline of the way the power relationships in counselling can be affected by the respective genders of client and counsellor. She draws attention to the 'social stereotype of the strong male doctor curing the weak female patient' (ibid.: 227) which can have an impact on the female client/male counsellor dyad, where the female client may be tempted to play a passive dependent role and the male counsellor a dominant, or protective, role. Where the client is male and the counsellor female, the power struggle can be felt quite strongly as the male client may feel a need to assert control of the situation arising from a dislike of being in the 'supplicant' role. When both parties are male, Chaplin says, there is potential for the stereotypical male competition for supremacy, and when both are female, there is the risk of the relationship sliding into something more cosy and intimate than formal counselling would sanction.

Over and above this I believe there are particular dangers for female counsellors and therapists precisely because of the history of gender relations, the preponderance of women in this field, and the very nature of the activities of counselling and therapy. The history of discrimination against women and their continuing fight for equality may lead a female counsellor or therapist to encourage (or suggest) a course of action for her female client primarily because it is in line with the wider ideals of the women's movement. In other words, a female counsellor who has a female client may be tempted, particularly when examining issues concerning relationships with men, to proselytize and lose sight of the client's unique circumstances. By the same token female counsellors may find themselves fiercely confronting what they perceive to be male clients' stereo-typical attitudes concerning gender relations. The counsellor/client dyad can thus become a battleground for gender relations rather than a therapeutic space for the client's self-exploration. The psychological theories which under-pin the enterprises of counselling and psychotherapy lay considerable emphasis on the desirability of attributes such as autonomy, independence, individuation and such like. These notions dovetail nicely with the aspirations of fem-inism and can lead to the dangerous assumption that any woman who is in a relationship where there is not total equality must automatically be frustrated and oppressed, and any man in a similar relationship is by definition auto-cratic and sexist. It is a short step from here to believing that your duty as a counsellor is to set things straight. As with anything else, counsellors and therapists need to work out their own values and establish what their gender means for them and their relationships. It is inappropriate and unethical to impose these values on clients.

Practitioners do, of course, need to be aware of the effect that the gender stereotyping inherent in our culture has had on their own perceptions, both of themselves and others. This awareness should play a conscious part in therapists' consideration of the response their clients invoke in them, and the response they, in turn, evoke in their clients. Similarly, therapists need to be aware of the impact of gen-der stereotyping on the client's world-view and his/her ability to connect with, express and examine their feelings, thoughts and emotions.

Counsellors and psychotherapists have a responsibility to gain a deep level of self-understanding. Part of this must be an awareness, for each person, of what it means to him or her to be a man or a woman in modern society. As part of any thorough training to become a counsellor or therapist, trainees should be invited to question their own assumptions about gender and the respective roles of men and women both towards each other and within society as a whole. There is a variety of assumptions which are prevalent and rarely challenged that can be detrimental to therapeutic work if the practitioner is lacking in self-awareness. Some of these assumptions are: women should be more giving and conciliatory than men; all people are psychologically better off if they are married, or at least in an intimate (heterosexual) relationship; women are only truly fulfilled if they have children; men are only truly fulfilled if they have a successful career. Of course, some of these assumptions may be true for some people, but the role of counsellor or therapist requires an openness to the different value systems with which people operate as well as a deep understanding of one's own.

Because of the preponderance of women in the field of counselling and therapy, and because of the 'feminine' nature of the attributes encouraged by counselling and psychotherapy training, there is a risk that 'masculine' attributes and qualities come to be denigrated, discounted and undervalued. In order for men to succeed within this field, as practitioners or clients, they have to demonstrate their ability to think and feel in ways that may be quite different from what has previously been expected of them. This is all very well, as long as it is not at the expense of 'male' qualities. Counselling and therapy are areas where 'female' language, values and styles of relating dominate. Those within the profession are generally enthusiastic about the idea of encouraging more men to train as counsellors and therapists, but, as Chris Rose points out, 'the condition sometimes seems to be that they are required not to behave as men' (Rose, 2002: 9). The challenge to counselling, she believes, is to recognize and redress this denigration of the male gender and its associated qualities. In this context it is men who are the marginalized group.

The need for an integration of masculine and feminine values and ways of thinking is held up as the way forward in this field (Chaplin, 1988; Lemma-Wright, 1995; Clare, 2000). What this comes down to is a celebration of difference and diversity (both within us and among us) rather than judging differences as either superior or inferior. Theorists as far back as Freud have pointed out the existence within all of us of both 'male' and 'female' attributes. It was Jung, however, who saw the recognition of the feminine and masculine aspects of the psyche, and the desirability of their integration, as the most important and challenging part of human development. Chaplin draws a parallel between the hierarchies within society and the hierarchical splits or tensions that operate within each one of us. Polarities exist between the desire for intimacy and the fear of rejection; between control and chaos; dependence and independence; power and powerlessness; perfection and uselessness (Chaplin, 1988: 50). We need to reconcile the opposites by realizing that they do not cancel each other out – we can have both. This, I believe, is what she means when she writes, 'Counselling needs to help people become more psychologically androgynous' (Chaplin, 1989: 236).

It is not necessarily androgyny which is the aim, rather a recognition of the individual needs, characteristics and attributes of both men and women. In order to achieve that we need to be able to acknowledge and embrace all aspects of our own psyches, in particular those parts which are stereotypically associated with the opposite gender from

100 | DIFFERENCE AND DISCRIMINATION

our own. Denigration of 'masculine' attributes if you are female, or 'feminine' attributes if you are male, is ultimately a denial of part of yourself. Self-knowledge, and the ability to facilitate others in their quest for greater self-understanding, is not achieved by denial but by the integration of the different components of our individual personalities.

4 | Sexuality

THE CONCEPT OF 'SEXUALITY' as part of human experience and behaviour as distinct from other areas of our experience is relatively modern. With this concept there comes the division of sexual behaviour into different types of activity: with partners of the same gender or the opposite gender; on one's own, with one partner, or more than one partner; activities involving different sexual positions and different parts of the anatomy. This in turn has generated numerous attempts to classify activities (either socially or legally) as acceptable or unacceptable, natural or unnatural, normal or abnormal.

The regulation of sexuality, by legislation, social opinion or both, led to the idea of people being identified, individually and in groups, by their sexual practices. The notion of possessing a heterosexual, homosexual or lesbian 'identity' is problematic for a number of reasons. It presupposes that each of us belongs exclusively to one group or the other. Furthermore, there is the assumption that by belonging to that group we automatically possess a number of characteristics common to all members of the group, other than our sexual preferences. Throughout history the western world has predominantly taken the view that sexual activity with a member of the opposite gender is 'normal' and 'natural' and that anything else is 'abnormal' and 'unnatural'. The proscriptions within this formulation have varied over time and place: whether or not such activity is sanctioned only within marriage or a stable relationship, what types of activity are acceptable, the expectations and assumptions around the relative roles (active or passive) of men and women, and so forth. At one time women of good social class were not expected to experience sexual pleasure, and any activity other than genital heterosexual intercourse was highly suspect. By the late twentieth century there was a widespread assumption that everyone, men and women, could or even should engage in a wide variety of sexual practices, provided these remained within the confines of legality. Not to do so, or not to experience regular orgasm, has come to be viewed by many as undesirable, unhealthy, or even psychologically damaging.

Despite this, there remains widespread discomfort with both male and female homosexuality. The sexual liberation of the 1960s and 1970s was decidedly heterosexual – it did little to change public opinion about same-sex relationships. It is disquieting to observe that among schoolchildren and adolescents the epithet 'gay' is a widely used term of abuse. In adult life people who identify themselves, or are identified by others, as homosexual or lesbian, are still widely stigmatized and discriminated against. The fact that a person's sexuality needs to be commented on – which is only the case if it is not heterosexual – is indicative of the prejudice around this area which is still endemic in our society. While I am aware that there are many other kinds of sexual behaviour for which people are stigmatized (transvestism, bisexuality, etc.), I will be focusing primarily on homosexuality and lesbianism which for too many people are still seen as representative of a sexuality which is in some way abnormal, alien or even sinful.

As with previous chapters, this chapter will begin with a historical overview of how differing sexual practices have been regarded and treated in different societies and at different times in history. This is followed by an examination of the theories that have arisen around attempts to explain homosexuality and lesbianism. The last section focuses on the problematic relationship between homosexuality and the enterprises of counselling and psychotherapy.

Homosexuality – a historical overview

The term 'homosexuality' was first used in 1868 in correspondence between a German-Hungarian journalist, Karl Maria Kertbeny, and the sexologist Karl Heinrich Ulrichs. It was adopted the following year by the medical sexual theorist, Dr Karl Westphals, and was being widely used in medical and psychiatric circles by the end of the nineteenth century. The term 'lesbian' was also first used, with its specific meaning of same-sex female sexuality, in a medical context, by Richard von Krafft-Ebing in his text *Psychopathia Sexualis* published in 1886. For some time after that lesbianism was commonly subsumed in the literature into the term 'homosexuality' which was taken to indicate male and female same-sex sexuality. 'Lesbian' did not enter widespread social use until the 1950s with the advent of the feminist movement. The term 'homosexuality' came into popular social use in the 1920s, preceding the invention of the term 'heterosexuality' in the 1930s. Since then the terms 'homosexuality' and 'heterosexuality' have become fixed in public opinion and medical terminology as identifying two separate and definitively different kinds of sexuality, practised by two separate and definitively different groups of people. Most pre-modern and non-western cultures did not differentiate human beings in this way; that is to say at the level of sexual preference. A person's sexual tastes were not ascribed to some positive, structural or definitive feature of his or her personality. However, the behaviour described by the term homosexuality has always been part of human sexual activity. The visual arts, literary, medical and religious texts of all historical periods abundantly demonstrate that human beings have desired, loved and had sex with members of their own gender throughout history.

Early history
There is a widely held belief that the society of Ancient Greece was an ideal world in which homosexual love and sexual activity was as acceptable as heterosexual relationships. There is some truth in this, but it is important to understand the social conventions that governed the sexual practices at that time. The distinction prevalent in Ancient Greece, and also in the Roman world, was between the 'active' and the 'passive' person in any sexual act, rather than the gender of the two persons. This distinction was viewed as vital as an indicator of superior or inferior social status. The convention for an adult male was to be the dominant partner in all sexual acts. What was not acceptable was to engage in anything that suggested effeminacy – in other words to be the submissive sexual partner. Sex was viewed as an activity characterized by domination rather than by mutuality. Adult male citizens in Athens and Rome, therefore, could have legitimate sexual relations with those of inferior social status – women, boys and slaves – but not with those of the same social status – other adult male citizens. In Greece the relationship between an adult male and his boy lover carried with it elements of mentoring; it was viewed as a recognizable stage of social development for a boy on his road to maturity. In both Athens and Rome the emphasis in sexuality was on social status as evidenced by being a freeborn citizen and demonstrated by taking a dominant sexual role. Both societies were male-dominated and in them, for sexual purposes, women and boys were seen as almost functionally interchangeable.

In later antiquity and, significantly, with the advent of Christianity, this view began to change dramatically. The idea emerged that only love between a man and a woman was natural and socially acceptable. The concept that men who love men and men who love women are separate and different begins to appear. Tolerance for homosexuality began to decrease in the first centuries of our era. Procreation came to be seen as the principal reason for sexual activity; consequently marriage became the fundamental social institution, the template for acceptable human and sexual relations. Early Christianity rejected homosexuality as unnatural, sinful and inimical to marriage. In God's 'natural order' there was no place for same-sex relationships – indeed they were seen as a violation of that order and automatically excluded the sinner from God's kingdom. By the fourth century AD homosexuality had become a moral crime as well as a sin, punishable by a variety of means including exile, castration, head-shaving, whipping and burning at the stake (Fone, 2000: 120).

Throughout the medieval period in the Christian world social opinion, endorsed by theological writings, viewed same-sex relationships as aberrant, shameful, sinful and unlawful. Few references are made in the literature of this time to lesbianism, though it was assumed to be included in the many laws proscribing homosexuality. In the numerous legal cases where homosexuality was brought to trial, only a handful involved a lesbian relationship. From the thirteenth century in Europe the death penalty was frequently invoked for acts of sodomy, which at various times was seen as infectious, politically suspect and indicative of heretical beliefs or treason. For a brief period during the Renaissance the glorification of classical writings produced a celebration, in literature at least, of male homosexuality or 'Greek love'. Despite this, the legal position remained unchanged, as did the view of the church. Between 1450 and 1650 'some of the most ferocious laws against sodomy were promulgated and more sodomites were executed than at any previous period of European history' (Fone, 2000: 214). In England the Ecclesiastical Courts held the power to punish those who transgressed the strict moral laws laid down by the church. Such transgressions included acts of 'sodomy' or 'buggery'. With the Reformation this situation changed – regulation of aberrant sexual practices was taken over by the state. In 1533 a law was passed which criminalized 'buggery'. It became a vice rather than (or as well as) a sin, and a crime carrying the death penalty. This situation persisted for the next 300 years.

Europe – the seventeenth to nineteenth centuries

The dominant view in Europe throughout the seventeenth and eighteenth centuries was that sex should be a means to an end. Procreation as its aim was seen as paramount. The family unit was the basis of society, and the man was the head of that unit. To be manly was to experience sexual desire only for women. While prostitution flourished and there was, in most countries, a tolerance of men who had sex outside marriage (though not an equal tolerance of the women with whom they had this illicit sex), the social attitude towards same-sex relationships remained hostile and condemnatory. Nevertheless there is ample evidence that such relationships took place. The emergence of a homosexual subculture is identified at about 1700 in many of the major European cities (Haussen, 1991; Trumbach, 1991; Weeks, 1991). By this time homosexual activity was viewed as forbidden and shameful behaviour of a deviant, effeminate minority of adult males; therefore the social control of this behaviour was seen as the task of the state. With the Enlightenment in the eighteenth century, however, there was a gradual decriminalization of sodomy in most parts of mainland Europe, bringing with it a removal of the death penalty. In England, by contrast, the pace of persecution and executions dramatically increased. England did not abandon the death penalty for sodomy until 1861 and homosexual acts remained criminal until well into the twentieth century. It is important to recognize that decriminalization, whenever it took place, did not mean social tolerance. Sodomy was still viewed, variously, as a disease, a vice, a deviation, a mortal sin and, above all, a bestial and unnatural act.

Nineteenth-century thought was characterized by a preoccupation with social and public order. Men and women were seen to have 'natural' characteristics and attributes that fitted them for particular tasks and for particular roles – social, economic and sexual. Nature was seen as the supreme example of the genuine and the immutable. It was believed that nature knew no vice and man should strive to get close to what was natural. The (erroneous) view that homosexuality did not exist in nature reinforced the belief that such behaviour was 'unnatural' and abnormal. Furthermore, homosexuality was seen as a threat to manliness and to the 'natural order' of things, and therefore to the whole social fabric. From early in the nineteenth century a link was made between immorality, sexual behaviour and disease. This appeared in the medical discourse of the time and was reinforced by the Christian ethic. Medical theory held (among other things) that masturbation led to homosexuality, which led to insanity, disease and death. It was widely believed that homosexuals could contaminate and 'infect' so-called 'normal' men. Victorian morality maintained that for men sexual desire was normal and natural, as long as its focus was women. For women the norm was seen as absence of sexual desire. As female heterosexual desire was denied, so female same-sex desire was unthinkable. Lesbianism, therefore, was socially invisible. But even for men the control of sexual passions was advocated as a safeguard against ill-health. These views reached their zenith towards the end of the century in the Purity movement, which was heavily informed by Christian ideals of moderation and prayer, and in a paternalistic middle-class evangelism towards the dissipated, animalistic and intellectually inferior lower classes.

Sexology and the medical model

In 1885 the first comprehensive law relating to male homosexuality was passed in England. The Criminal Law Amendment Act used the dangerously vague term 'gross indecency' and in effect made all homosexual acts illegal. By this time the term 'homosexuality' had come into use, originating as we have seen in a medical context. This was the period when scientific determinism was at its height, characterized by the desire to classify, categorize and find a place for everything and everyone in what was perceived to be a conflicting and changing world. Darwinian theory distinguished between sexual selection and natural selection; that survival depended on sexual selection leant weight to the burgeoning scientific and medical interest in the nature and causes of different sexual behaviours. The new discipline of sexology led to the invention of the terms 'invert' and 'pervert' and, more significantly, to the notion of sexuality as a means of defining an individual. Richard von Krafft-Ebing's work *Psychopathia Sexualis*, published in 1886, was an attempt to categorize people by their sexual practices. He listed a huge array of sexual perversions and abnormalities. The fundamental premiss to his work and that of other sexologists was that heterosexual object choice was the natural and normal state. Anything else fell into the category of perversity. Krafft-Ebing defined homosexuality as an absence of 'normal sexual feeling' and saw its cause as mental 'degeneration' (Fone, 2000: 275).

This was the beginning of the debate about innate and acquired sexual characteristics and preferences which continues to this day. The focus in much of the sexological writings is on male homosexuality, with the search for explanations or causes centred on biology. There was, however, a recognition of the existence of lesbianism, which was, like male homosexuality, viewed as degenerate and deviant. However, the existence of same-sex female desire and sexuality was a particular challenge to paternalistic

Victorian morality and the social role assigned to women. How could a woman find satisfaction, either sexual or emotional, with anyone other than a man? Attempts to explain lesbianism, therefore, focused more on social than sexual behaviour, linking lesbianism with a misguided rejection of the conventional female role, or seeing it as a result of the lamentable increase in female education and political involvement. However, the legal situation created by the 1885 Act did not apply to women. An attempt to extend the provisions of this Act to women was made in 1921. This failed, partly at least on the grounds that publicity about lesbianism would only serve to make more women aware of its existence. Invisibility and denial have always been a central part of the social response to lesbianism.

The medicalization of homosexuality brought about by the scientific determinism and sexological theories of the late nineteenth century added pathology to the list of definitions of same-sex sexual desire. Viewed historically as a sin, a crime, a vice and a disease, it now became a pathological biological condition by which a person could be defined as separate and different from the norm. In his book *Coming Out: Homosexual Politics in Britain from the Nineteenth Century to the Present* (1977), Jeffrey Weeks reflects on the fact that homosexuality has existed throughout history, but that what has varied has been the ways in which it has been regarded and defined by different societies. He distinguishes between homosexual behaviour which is 'universal' and homosexual identity which he calls 'historically specific' (Weeks, 1977: 3). The late nineteenth and early twentieth centuries saw the invention of the notion of sexual identity, with homosexuality seen as an aberration, and the term 'heterosexuality' coined to define what was viewed as the natural and normal state. Thus the sexual practices a person engaged in became the means whereby they were identified as individuals. Psychoanalysis served only to reinforce this trend. Freud's theories on sexuality in general, and homosexuality in particular, will be discussed in the next section. Suffice to say here that broadly speaking he was singing the same tune as the sexologists. Whereas Freud's theories indubitably present at times a more open and controversial picture of the nature of human sexuality, his successors adopted an orthodox stance in which anything other than heterosexuality was viewed as indicative of incomplete or distorted psychological development and consequently as perverse.

The twentieth century

At the beginning of the twentieth century there was little organized resistance to the prevailing homophobic social attitude. However, networks of subcultures of gay men and lesbian women were growing in both Europe and the USA. For many the notion of sexual identity became a means of self-definition – this was what eventually blossomed into the individual and collective resistance of the Gay Liberation Movement. Two world wars had the effect of expanding the sense of homosexual unity on both sides of the Atlantic. Old social structures and values were challenged or changed and men and women were either mobilized or involved in war work which took them outside their local communities. At the same time, in the nations on both sides of the global conflict, war produced a xenophobic strain of homophobia as sexual difference was conflated with betrayal of a nation's values. In Germany the Nazi regime targeted homosexuals, along with other minority groups, viewing such aberrant behaviour as contaminating and corrupting the Aryan race and, like the Jews, endangering its survival. Mosse reports that between 10,000 and 20,000 homosexuals died in the concentration camps (Mosse, 1985: xx).

By the end of the Second World War homosexuality had become an issue exposed to social, medical and scientific discussion. As a group, homosexuals were becoming more visible – and as such widely exposed to social ostracism. The Kinsey report, published in the USA in 1948, was an attempt to cast some light on the nature of sexuality in men. Kinsey claimed that 37 per cent of the male popula-tion of the United States had some homosexual experience between adolescence and old age and that between 4 per cent and 10 per cent of American men were exclusively homo-sexual. The implications of Kinsey's work were that homosexuality was widespread and, more controversially, that it was a normal and healthy form of sexual expression. This attempt to foster a more liberal view had the unfortu-nate effect of provoking enormous public moral outrage. In England there was a heavy social and police crackdown on homosexuality around this time. Prosecutions and convic-tions frequently led to enforced psychiatric treatment in an attempt to 'cure' what was seen as a dangerous perversion. Treatment included aversion therapy, lobotomy, electric shock treatment, castration and hormone and drug therapy (Jeffery-Poulter, 1991: 14, 51). In the USA the homosexual witch-hunt acquired political overtones. McCarthy's investigation of suspected communists in government linked the politically suspect with the sexually suspect and the notion of the homosexual as a political menace was added to the stereotype. A similar phenomenon took place in the UK with the defection of Guy Burgess and Donald Maclean to the Soviet Union, an event which fuelled para-noia about homosexuality, associating it with disloyalty, treachery and treason.

Many commentators see the persecution of homosexuals in the 1950s as the spur to the creation of the modern homosexual rights movement (Weeks, 1985; D'Emilio, 1991; Jeffery-Poulter, 1991; Fone, 2000). For the first time it was argued that homosexuals should be seen as a minor-ity group and therefore viewed within the discourse of civil liberties and human rights rather than within the confines of social morality or medical diagnosis. Prejudice against homosexuality, however, was and still is deeply rooted. From the mid-1950s to the mid-1970s there were radical changes in attitudes to sex and sexual behaviour in the western world. Despite that, traditional attitudes have been persistent including the continued discrimination of sexual 'deviants'. The so-called 'sexual revolution' was predominantly sexist and heterosexist. But homosexuality had found a voice and changes began, albeit slowly. The Stonewall Rebellion in New York in 1969, following a police raid on a gay bar, led to the birth of Gay Activism in the USA which soon spread to England and mainland Europe. In England in 1967 homosexual acts in private between consenting males over the age of twenty-one were decriminalized. Scotland and Northern Ireland followed suit in 1980. In 1973 the American Psychiatric Association removed homosexuality from their list of sexual disorders, primarily as a result of social pressure rather than scientific reassessment. It took a long time for similar changes in the UK to be effected, homosexuality remaining in the ICD classification of mental disorders until 1992. To this day both countries continue to have diagnoses such as 'gender identity disorder' within their classification systems – an indication that the medicalization of homosexuality and lesbianism has never fully disappeared.

Since the 1980s there have been huge changes in social attitudes to homosexuality. The terms 'gay' and 'lesbian' have widely come into use, 'homosexual' being largely rejected by those to whom it is applied due to its medical and diagnostic origins. The numbers of pubs and clubs which accept gay men and lesbian women have increased from the late 1970s and many people in public and political office have become able to acknowledge their homosexuality openly without losing their jobs. The development of the feminist and gay liberation movements empowered lesbian women and gay men to speak out and 'come out'. But despite a growing climate of toleration, many saw these trends as threats to old values and the traditional family unit. 'Family values' as expounded by the politics and social policies of Reagan and Thatcher continued to be vaunted as the epitome of social and moral purity. Such values were, by definition, heterosexual and patriarchal and anything outside that was by implication denigrated and devalued.

The advent of AIDS in the mid-1980s accentuated these deeply ingrained prejudices. AIDS happened at a time when the revolution in the gay world was incomplete. Jeffrey Weeks makes the distinction between the homosexual who at this time was 'partially accepted' and homosexuality which was still eschewed (Weeks, 1985: 45). AIDS acquired a particular moral stigma because it was associated with a group of people who were already marginalized and disapproved of. It provoked widespread moral panic and was seen by many as retribution for unhealthy, immoral or perverted sexual practices. Jeffery-Poulter (1991) details the social and political reaction to AIDS in the UK, highlighting the fact that there was little public concern until heterosexuals became infected. While large sums of public money were given for haemophiliac AIDS sufferers, pitifully small amounts were given for gay men who had the disease. The gay community was scapegoated; while they themselves 'deserved' illness, they were pilloried for putting other 'innocent' victims at risk. AIDS had the effect of reviving lingering beliefs in homosexuality as a disease and, moreover, one which was infectious. Homophobia increased dramatically with calls for the re-criminalization and imprisonment of homosexuals. Homosexuals were seen as carriers of disease, potential corrupters of the nation's youth and as child molesters. Within this climate the infamous Section 28 of the Local Government Act was passed in 1988, prohibiting the promotion of homosexuality in schools. This reflected public anxiety about the stability of the family and the need to protect society against the moral decay that, for many, homosexuality had come to represent. Section 28 had the effect of producing an unprecedented display of gay and lesbian solidarity and provoked the establishment of organizations by the gay community to lobby the media and the legal and parliamentary systems.

Prior to this there had been a lack of unity between lesbian women and gay men as their aims and aspirations had diverged throughout the twentieth century. In the early part of this period female sexuality was seen primarily in the context of the heterosexual family and male dominance. Lesbianism was largely invisible in the public consciousness and in the legal sense. This was in effect a denial of female sexuality as much as of lesbianism. With the advent of the women's movement this situation was changed dramatically. For many women within this movement lesbianism was seen as the ultimate expression of female solidarity and the rejection of male oppression. Lesbianism thus acquired a political as well as a sexual dimension. Many lesbians left the male-dominated Gay Liberation Front in the 1970s to join the women's movement and adopted a separatist stance. Like gay men, lesbians gained little from the sexual revolution of the 1960s and 1970s, but, unlike gays, they were little affected by AIDS. However, they were, by implication, included in the public condemnation of non-heterosexual sexual relations following the outbreak of AIDS and were united with the male gay community in their outrage at the implications of Section 28.

The contemporary situation
The last decade of the twentieth century saw a significant rise in violence against homosexuals. As the gay community has become more visible and more vocal, the result has been a homophobic backlash rather than greater tolerance. Homosexuality has continued to be seen as both a sin and

a disease, homosexuals as both ill and immoral – a logical impossibility. Thus homosexuality is something you can be born with, seduced into, or catch from someone else. As Halperin points out, in these terms heterosexuality becomes by definition, at the same time a natural condition, a highly laudable accomplishment and a precarious state that can be overthrown by contact with an unscrupulous homosexual seducer (Halperin, 1998: 263). Public perception of homosexuality has become illogical and confused, conflating paedophilia, homosexuality and mental illness. Incidents of sexual abuse of children and the exposure of paedophile rings, which have received wide media coverage, have only served to add to this confusion. Homosexual men are widely believed to be dangerously predatory, putting at risk all boys or young men with whom they come into contact. The confusion between homosexuality and paedophilia creates public suspicion of any gay man whose job involves working with young children. And yet the vast majority of cases of child sex abuse are perpetrated not by homosexuals but by heterosexuals.

In Europe and the USA homosexuality is no longer either illegal or classified as a mental illness. However, there remain many areas of law which are discriminatory of same-sex relationships. In the UK in particular changes in the law have been slow; declassification as a psychiatric disorder only coming in 1992, and the ban on homosexuality within the armed forces finally being lifted in 1999. The age of consent for homosexuals in England was reduced from twenty-one to eighteen in 1994, whereas for heterosexuals it is sixteen. England, unlike many other European countries and some states in the USA and Canada, does not yet recognize same-sex partnerships in law. This has implications for a number of areas where gays and lesbians are disadvantaged: pensions, fringe benefits, inheritance, tax, and transfer of property. They are not recognized as next of kin which can cause complications in matters such as illness and death – only next of kin are consulted by hospitals and health professionals and only they have the right to make funeral arrangements. In many of these legal matters same-sex couples are in the same position as unmarried hetero-sexual couples, the difference being that the latter can choose to marry whereas the former cannot. The situation is changing. Some companies do now offer fringe benefits and pension rights to same-sex partners, and in 2001 changes were made to the Criminal Injuries Scheme which extended eligibility for fatal awards in the same way. In November 2002 a gay man won the right to take over a dead partner's tenancy, setting an important precedent in this area. At the same time gay (and unmarried) couples won the right to adopt, a decision that was greeted by wide-spread public concern.

Within the gay community the philosophy that is increas-ingly being adopted by gay men and lesbian women is that of gay rights as human and civil rights. In the USA this has already proved problematic; in many states the courts have ruled that homosexuals possess no rights as a minority group because homosexuality (unlike race or gender) is not an 'immutable characteristic' (Halperin, 1998: 255). Although the post-AIDS backlash is subsiding, and toler-ance is once more on the increase, it is an uneasy tolerance, tinged with the 'political correctness' of the late twentieth century, and a far cry from true and universal acceptance. At the beginning of the twenty-first century many openly gay men and lesbian women are pursuing successful careers in various spheres of public and political life, but there are still large areas of the establishment where the merest hint of homosexuality leads to disgrace and dis-missal. The most recent area which has been widely exposed to scrutiny in this regard is the Church. In 2003 the issue of openly gay clergymen being appointed to high office has created worldwide schisms within the Anglican community. In the UK Canon Jeffrey John, an openly gay priest, declined the offer of the Bishopric of Reading, following weeks of bitter argument over his sexuality within the Anglican Church. In the US, however, Gene Robinson was successfully appointed as Bishop of New Hampshire. His appointment provoked an emergency summit of all the primates of the Anglican Church to discuss the issue of homosexuality and the Church's attitude towards it.

In the twenty-first century a significant number of gay men and lesbian women have 'come out' publicly but they are still in the minority – many more lead lives where an important part of who they are and what they experience is kept hidden. Lesbians and gay men are still consistently victimized in schools, colleges and universities, and discriminated against in the workplace. They frequently lack the support of their families and are at higher risk of stress-related illnesses, depression and suicide. All too often they remain trapped in secret double lives because of the all-pervading nature of the homophobia endemic in our society.

Sexuality and homosexuality – some of the theories

An individual's sexual preference, unlike their gender, skin colour or race, is not visible at birth. It is, by contrast, something that manifests itself over time, usually becoming apparent as the person reaches, or approaches, adolescence and sexual maturity. As many studies have shown, beginning with Alfred Kinsey's texts in 1948 and 1953 (Kinsey, Pomeroy and Martin, 1948; 1953), to engage in same-sex sexual activity is common among people who also engage in opposite-sex sexual activity, many of whom will then develop a pattern of exclusively opposite-sex sexual activity. This calls into question the validity of identifying a group of people by a type of behaviour which is by no means exclusive to that particular group. As Foucault (1976) pointed out, the use of language to create sexual categories – homosexual, heterosexual, transvestite, and so on – by which we then regulate and categorize sexuality, is an imposition of a structure upon human experience which may not exist within the experience itself. In other words, by inventing terms like heterosexual and homosexual we are making divisions between groups of people and the activities they engage in which are intrinsically artificial.

Nevertheless, the history of sexuality, homosexuality and lesbianism reveals that the advent of scientific and medical research provoked a desire to find the cause or reason for what was perceived to be a significant difference in an area of human behaviour from the assumed norm. It may be that the question 'what causes homosexuality?' is spurious. However, it was a question that was asked, and continues to be asked. A variety of answers has been posited, and along the way many have challenged the validity of both the question and the various answers. An essential part of this debate is played by those to whom the various theories have been applied; how they perceive themselves in relation to their sexuality and sexual practices, and in relation to the theories about their sexuality and the response this incites in society at large.

Essentialism versus constructivism
As with so many debates about the nature of human characteristics one of the central questions focuses on whether homosexuality is an innate characteristic, present at birth but not yet apparent, or whether it is in some way learned, acquired or chosen – the product of environmental or social influences.

The sexologists were in the forefront of this debate. Their aim was to discover and analyse what they saw as 'the laws of nature'. Krafft-Ebing defined the 'natural instinct' as male sexuality whose natural object was the opposite sex (Weeks, 1985: 69). Heterosexuality was *a priori* taken as the biological norm and all other sexual practices were defined as abnormal or perverse. For the sexologists sex is seen as an essentially biological force, a natural process and therefore innate in the individual man or woman. The definitions put forward in their works are fundamentally medical, with considerable emphasis on the physical and behavioural manifestations of the various categories of behaviour. Some made distinctions between innate and acquired homosexuality; the term 'invert' was used to define those believed to be genetically different, the term 'pervert' reserved for those whose moral weakness led them to indulge in homosexual behaviour. 'Inversion', a congenital state, was largely viewed as a defect, the result of genetic abnormality or physical trauma, resulting in a condition comparable with mental illness or insanity. The early sexologists' attempt to explain sexuality in terms of the 'sexual instinct' raised the question of the focus of that instinct. Bound as they were to ideas of nature, they saw the only proper aim as reproduction. Women's sexuality, if acknowledged at all, could then be respectably explained as a product of the 'maternal instinct'. Sexual variations, therefore, become failures of heterosexuality. It has been pointed out, however, that such a theory does not explain the greater part of heterosexual sexual activity, only a small proportion of which is activated by the desire to reproduce or parent (Weeks, 1985; Spinelli, 2001).

The sexologists' mission to find the truth about sex and sexual differences in biology, nature and the instincts has continued to the present day. With the further development of scientific research in the twentieth century, sexual essentialism has focused more on chromosomes and hormones, DNA and genetics. Sociobiology, founded by E.O. Wilson, proposed a synthesis between sociology and genetics. It attempts to do this by finding a genetic basis for all human behaviour, on the premise that all characteristics that survive are adaptive and therefore serve a function. Genetic determinism is thus seen as the explanation for all human characteristics and social behaviour; within this framework sexual practices are seen as 'bonding devices' as well as a means of procreation, and homosexuality is explained in terms of aiding the evolutionary process by providing 'helpers' within the social group (Wilson, 1975: 555). This is an interesting hypothesis in the light of the social ostracism to which homosexuals have widely been subjected in western societies. In the late twentieth century the focus has been on the science of genetics rather than its sociological implications, with attempts to isolate differences in the X chromosome as the 'cause' of homosexuality (Hamer, 1994). While many (Rose et al., 1984; Satinover, 1998) refute the logic of a genetic cause for homosexuality, research into the genome, and its accompanying attempt to isolate specific human characteristics within particular genes, has gained a momentum which is unlikely to be easily stopped. The history of scientific and medical research would suggest that even if/when no biological or genetic link is found, theorists committed to the existence of such would remain undaunted. Philosophically it is impossible to prove that something does *not* exist.

A challenge to essentialism comes in the form of a refutation of the reductionism that it represents. It is argued that the view of sexuality offered by the sexologists and biologists is too narrow, too rigid and in many ways misses the point entirely. Foucault, for example, sees sexuality as a 'historical construct' which is far wider and more complex than notions of instincts or procreative aims. An alternative to the biological view suggests that sexual definitions such as homosexuality are socially constructed, a way of categorizing people, the need for which arises from the impulse for social organization and the establishment of norms and stereotypes. As Jeffrey Weeks puts it, 'there exists a plurality of sexual desires, of potential ways of life, and of relationships' (Weeks, 1985: 10). These are not given credence in the essentialist view, except in terms of definition and regulation. Many modern commentators tend towards the view of homosexuality as a choice. It is important to distinguish here between homosexual activity and homosexual identity. To identify oneself as homosexual or lesbian is indeed a personal choice, one motivated by, among other things, political or social factors. The fact that many people who identify themselves as heterosexual do at some time in their lives engage in homosexual behaviour is put forward as an argument for seeing homosexuality not as an irreversible, exclusive condition, but as a choice which, some would argue, is an unhealthy and injurious one (Satinover, 1998), and can be changed. This is countered by the view that homosexuality should be seen as an expression, like other expressions, of human sexuality, which can manifest itself in a rich variety of ways, no one way being necessarily better or worse than any other.

The view that sexuality should be understood as a continuum or spectrum directly challenges the bipolarity inherent in the heterosexual/homosexual dichotomy. It also calls into question the notion of a fixed sexual orientation – a challenge which is supported by experience and observation. Single-sex institutions – prisons, boarding schools, religious orders, the armed forces – have long been recognized as places where a high level of homosexual activity takes place without any or all of the participants necessarily continuing with an exclusively homosexual life-style once outside the institution. Davies and Neal (1996) point out that many people who define themselves as heterosexual have sex with their own gender and that many more have dreams or fantasies about doing so. Similarly, many lesbians and gay men have sex with the opposite gender and yet continue to define themselves as lesbian or gay. Weeks defines the 'homosexual component' as 'an aspect of the body's sexual possibilities' and continues that the 'possibilities of homosexuality and heterosexuality are socially structured limitations in the flux of potentialities developed in the process of emotional socialization' (Weeks, 1991: 44). The nature of sexual identity is central to the discussion of what those limitations are and how they affect an individual's own understanding of his or her sexuality. But before proceeding with that, it is important to examine the contribution of psychoanalysis to the debate.

Freud and the post-Freudians

Freud was writing at the time when sexology and the study of sexual 'perversions' were at their height. His theories about sexuality are fundamentally rooted in biology and tend towards the determinist end of the spectrum. However, there is in Freud's theories a rather more liberal and tolerant attitude towards aberration than is often recognized – a tolerance that disappeared in the formulations of his successors. There are also, as with so many of Freud's ideas, ambiguities in his view on homosexuality.

For Freud the starting point is polymorphous perversity. The human infant begins life as innately bisexual – perversity is thus seen as something which is present in all people, from which there is a circuitous path to reach the point of adult heterosexual desire. In Freud's view, 'the disposition to perversions is itself of no great rarity but must form part of what passes as normal constitution' (Freud, 1905: 86). He deliberately severs the connection between the sexual instinct and heterosexual genitality, seeing the latter as something which is achieved through a complex process of development, rather than something which is pre-given. Thus so-called normal sexuality is not an *a priori* aspect of human nature – 'the exclusive sexual interest felt by men for women is also a problem that needs elucidating and is not a self-evident fact' (ibid.: 57, n. 1). Within this formulation, homosexuality becomes a variant of sexual life. Indeed Freud wrote that everyone has the capacity for homosexual object choice: 'in addition to their manifest heterosexuality, a very considerable measure of latent or unconscious homosexuality can be detected in all normal people' (Freud, 1920: 399).

Despite all this, Freud does have a normative view of psychosexual development. He saw homosexuality as the consequence of an 'arrest' in normal sexual development. The implication from this is that full maturity has not been achieved in that the (for Freud) essential stages of the oedipus complex have not been passed through. So, although Freud saw *all* sexuality as a restriction in object choice, and condemned the view of homosexuality as a vice or a crime, he clearly viewed heterosexuality as the normal or desirable outcome of psychosexual development. It was this aspect of his theory that passed into psychoanalytic orthodoxy. Later psychoanalytic theorists stress the 'natural' course of heterosexuality, seeing homosexuality as a perversion and a deviation from the norm (Chodorow, 1994). This became so much a dominant view that by 1962 an eminent psychoanalyst was able to say, 'all psychoanalytic theories assume that adult homosexuality is psychopathologic' (Izzard, 2000). The more tolerant view of homosexuality present in Freud's early writings had by then largely disappeared.

Whether homosexuality is seen as an essential part of a person's being, or as a characteristic that is acquired, learned or chosen, has a significant impact on the view that society has of those identified as homosexual. Adopting an essentialist view leads in two directions. If homosexuality is biological – genetic, hormonal or in some other way physical – then that opens the way to abusive forms of psychosurgery, drug therapy, genetic modification or even eugenics. On the other hand, an inborn trait absolves the individual from responsibility – one cannot be blamed or punished for a characteristic comparable with the colour of your eyes or an aptitude for sport. Seeing sexual orientation as fixed and immutable puts minority sexual groups on the same footing as other minority groups in regard to demanding equal civil and human rights.

A constructionist view, meanwhile, offers a different picture. If homosexuality is seen as a choice, then clearly the individual is personally responsible for making that choice. This also takes us in two, conflicting directions. It raises the issue of human freedom in the context of the right to make individual choices and adopt individual life-styles, even if they are different from the perceived norm. It also causes moral panic at the prospect of other people, especially the young, being indoctrinated into a way of life that many perceive as unnatural and unhealthy. If, however, homosexuality is viewed as the result of a complex combination of psychological and environmental influences, it becomes something for which the individual cannot really be blamed, but which could be amenable to change. This brings us back to various forms of psychological treatment, aversion therapy, drug therapy, and the like.

It is these considerations which, among other things, have had an impact on the concept of sexuality as an identity, and the positions adopted by gay and lesbian activists in their struggle against discrimination.

Sexual identity
The idea of sexual identity began with the sexologists in the late nineteenth and early twentieth centuries. The notion that what you did, in terms of your sexual activity and preferences, determined what sort of person you were, divided people into separate categories by which they were defined. This is seen by many as a spurious or even deliberately manipulative concept, with no basis in the reality of human experience, or, as Weeks puts it, 'a crude tactic of power designed to obscure a real sexual diversity with the myth of sexual destiny' (Weeks, 1991: 74). However, homosexuals have themselves accepted this identity as a way of self-definition and a means of individual and collective resistance. It has provided a sense of social location, which has been both liberating and validating to people who have been consistently stigmatized and persecuted by society. The attacks on sexual deviants in the 1950s and 1960s had the

effect of consolidating this sense of identity, and it became an essential part of the gay movement in the late 1960s. In order to campaign for civil rights it is imperative for a group to 'present' as unified round a common factor. Homosexuality as an identity provided that unifying rallying-point. The difficulty that then arises is that it becomes problematic to challenge the notion of a fixed sexual orientation without undermining the achievements and forward momentum of the movement for equality and recognition. This is the tension that exists within the gay and lesbian community to this day. Many within that community reject the connotations of sexual identity that suggest something static and unchangeable; they also reject the associated assumption that they are a homogeneous group who share other characteristics apart from their sexual preferences.

Moreover, not all people who are inclined towards homosexual behaviour wish to embrace a homosexual identity. The latter has become as much a statement of life-style and of a political commitment as of sexual preference. The term 'gay' is used by many to indicate this separation. It is an attempt to depart from the medical underpinnings of the designation 'homosexual' and indicate choice in all areas of human existence. Modern gay identity is as much a political as a personal or social identity, with no necessary relationship between sexual practice and sexual identity. The reaction against being defined solely or primarily on the basis of one's sexuality is becoming increasingly apparent in the contemporary gay community. The politically correct collective term has become 'lesbian, gay, bisexual, transgendered and friends', and the suggestion has been made that, having broadened it thus far, we might as well adopt the term 'sexual beings' and forget the distinctions altogether (Queen and Schimel, 1997). Sexuality, be it homosexual, heterosexual or any-other-sexual is seen as being about diversity, change and choice, and the concept of sexual identity negates that choice by trying to proscribe and fix people within a limited range of behaviour and experience.

The tension between sexual identity and sexual practice has been an intrinsic part of lesbianism throughout the twentieth century. With the advent of the feminist movement lesbianism became for many women a political statement. The point of protest – that heterosexual sex for women is viewed as male domination – does not exist for gay men. But feminism and lesbianism are not coterminous. There is a separation between on the one hand those who identify themselves as lesbians, but who see themselves as politically feminist and would understand their lesbianism to be an expression of that political commitment, and on the other hand those who identify as lesbians but whose political expression is not feminism – for them lesbianism *is* about sex. The difficulty with lesbian identity as a political statement is that it quickly moves away from anything even vaguely sexual towards ideas of female solidarity, independence and sisterhood. The danger here is the denial of female sexuality altogether, which undermines the notion of *sexual* lesbianism, a notion that for many is a vital part of both their experience and how they view themselves within the context of their sexuality.

Debate about the nature of homosexuality continues within scientific, medical and political spheres and within the gay community itself. As with many other minority groups, the emphasis from those within the group is on demands for acceptance of who they are in all aspects of their lives and beings. While solidarity is achieved by uniting under a common banner, individual lesbian women and gay men are increasingly challenging the assumptions of homogeneity that homosexual and lesbian 'identity' carries with it. For many heterosexuals, however, it is more comfortable to keep homosexuality as the characteristic of a distinct 'other' group, and to theorize about it as a separate and different condition. Such theories serve to maintain the 'norm' of heterosexuality and to retain the illusion of a divide between the two groups. This divide perpetuates the notion that same-sex sexual relations are only practised by the 'other' group – gay men and lesbian women. To challenge this idea would be profoundly uncomfortable and disturbing for many people who identify themselves as heterosexual.

Homosexuality in counselling and psychotherapy

Within the enterprises of counselling and psychotherapy there has always been a specific difficulty in relationship to sexuality in that, as we have seen, the classical theory underlying much therapeutic and counselling practice divides sexuality into specific orientations and regards anything other than exclusive heterosexuality as a perversion or as in some way an aberration of the norm. This has led in the past to difficulties for gay men and lesbian women who wish to undergo psychotherapy or counselling training, as well as to practices within the profession where clients who present with sexual orientations other than heterosexual are subjected to attempts to 'cure' them of their sexual leanings. Such practices are, thankfully, rare today, but there remains a legacy of viewing homosexuality as in some way pathological, in particular within psychodynamic and psychoanalytic models. Even where such a view is absent, the 'otherness' of gay or lesbian sexuality is experienced by many counsellors and therapists as faintly alarming, disturbing or distasteful. Such responses, acknowledged or denied, can clearly have a significant impact on both the therapeutic relationship and the outcome of the work.

The experience of being homosexual

In order for a therapist to be able to empathize with his or her client there needs to be some understanding of what it is like to inhabit that client's world. With a gay or lesbian client it is vital to have some understanding of the various components and manifestations of homophobia.

Discrimination and persecution of sexual minorities is inextricably linked with the gender stereotypes that are central to our culture, these stereotypes being founded in heterosexism – the assumption that heterosexuality is the only acceptable and viable life option. Such an arrangement reinforces the idea of the 'manly' man – dominant, assertive, in command, and so forth – and the 'feminine' woman – passive, dependent and in need of protection. Because gay men and lesbian women breach these stereotypes they are seen as a threat to the established order – and in particular to the patriarchy in which men and 'masculine' values are dominant. It is for this reason, as history reveals, that the social and legal focus has been more on male homosexuals than on lesbians. Even in Ancient Greece the emphasis was on the dominant (that is, masculine) nature of a sexual act, and in modern times the focus of police surveillance and arrests has been male homosexual activity almost exclusively.

The emphasis on gender conformity begins very early in life, with girls and boys expected to behave in ways appropriate to their gender. It is striking, however, that gender non-conformity in boys attracts significantly more negative attention than in girls. Little girls are permitted, generally speaking, to play rough games, wear trousers and behave like 'tomboys'. Boys, on the other hand, who act in any way that is perceived to be 'girlish' or 'effeminate' are corrected very quickly. As we have seen, however, the counterpart of this for girls and women is the 'invisibility' of lesbianism, which is part of the general repression and denial of women's sexuality. In her analysis of homophobia, Karen Franklin puts forward the notion that 'homosexuals are viewed as culturally threatening more because they are perceived as violating essential gender norms than because they violate sexual taboos' (Franklin, 1998: 11).

Another central element of homophobia which is frequently cited is that of repressed homosexuality. If we view sexuality, in all its manifestations, as a continuum of different expressions and behaviours of which we are all potentially capable, then the imposition of strict sexual identities and categories poses a problem for all of us. What do we do with those elements of our sexuality which do not fit our personal identification? The argument goes that we repress any socially deviant tendencies which then lend extra weight to the condemnation and persecution of those who openly identify themselves as deviant – in this case, homosexual. An extreme form of this view would see the so-called normal person as the one who is sick and disturbed because he or she represses all but their heterosexual desire, a process which produces an anxiety and paranoia which is then projected onto others (Archer and Lloyd, 1985). This would seem to be borne out by evidence that negative attitudes towards gay men and lesbian women are associated with people who tend to hold rigid, traditional and conservative views in other spheres, including non-permissive attitudes towards sex and traditional or oppressive views regarding the roles of women (Simon, 1998). Such people are the least likely to have identified or accepted those components of their own sexuality which fall outside the heterosexual norm.

Homophobia manifests itself further in the stereotypes that are culturally prevalent about homosexuals themselves. They are seen as promiscuous, dishonest, predatory, incapable of committed or sustained relationships, corrupters of children and unsuitable as parents. Same-sex relationships, being non-procreative, are viewed as primarily sexual in nature, a characteristic not commonly attributed to heterosexual relationships. The more lesbian women and gay men present as 'stereotypical', that is, as butch or effeminate, the more negative attention they attract. The current social situation seems to be one where gays and lesbians are tolerated by society as long as they remain relatively invisible. This presents a personal dilemma for each lesbian and gay person. By remaining 'closeted' there is less likelihood of encountering direct discrimination. But long-term concealment of an aspect of who you are is itself very stressful. Many lesbian and gay people feel they need to 'pass' as heterosexual at least some of the time in order to keep their jobs or maintain a particular social position. Consequently they inhabit two different worlds, living in constant fear of being exposed and rejected.

For the gay or lesbian person one of the effects of being brought up in a world dominated by heterosexist attitudes is the creation of an internal negative self-image. From early childhood we are exposed to anti-homosexual biases that are sanctioned by western culture. The realization that they are different from the social norms and are negatively regarded by society can cause lesbian women and gay men to incorporate these negative feelings into their self-image, resulting in internalized homophobia. This can range from self-doubt to overt self-hatred and is implicated in the high incidence of depression and suicide among young homosexuals (DiPlacido, 1998). An alternative response is one of denial – the construction of a self-image which excludes the label 'lesbian' or 'gay', regardless of one's sexual practices. This psychological 'split' is a type of self-deception and can lead to heightened distress when faced with negative social responses. Such a stance is not conducive to self-acceptance and is stressful to maintain on a long-term basis.

The process of 'coming out' is widely regarded as pivotal to psychological health and well-being, though it must be remembered that this is an individual choice, and a path eschewed by many. Central to this process is the response, or imagined response, of the individual's family. Unequivocal delight is unlikely to be the response. Even where there is acceptance and support there is usually an element of ambivalence, and for many the major or sole source of support is the lesbian and gay community rather than family members. Similarly the response of friends, colleagues and employers can have a big impact on the individual who may have to re-evaluate dramatically many social and professional relationships.

Gay men and lesbian women are constantly and continuously confronted by homophobia. Anti-homosexual attitudes manifest as rejection by friends, colleagues or family, in violent assaults and in discrimination in housing, employment, entitlements and basic civil rights. Lesbians and gays must constantly monitor their surroundings and the safety or otherwise of any situation they are in. They are very careful about displaying affection to same-sex lovers in public. A heterosexual relationship is celebrated and acknowledged by family and friends; it is socially acceptable for the couple to acknowledge openly their love for each other. A lesbian or gay couple, however, are expected to keep their affections and affairs out of the public eye. Social tolerance is very thin – the underlying condemnation and fear of difference is never very far away.

Counselling and therapy with gay and lesbian clients

Although most current models of psychotherapy and counselling do not teach students that homosexuality is an illness or a perversion, there is nevertheless a strongly heterosexist bias in the developmental models that are included in training. Freud's psychosexual stages of development and Eriksson's eight-stage model frequently form the backbone of counselling training programmes. Both of these take heterosexual development as the norm; thus individual human development, sex, gender, couples, family and relationship issues are all explored and discussed solely within a heterosexual context. Most British counselling and psychotherapy training programmes do not include specific input on working with gay or lesbian clients as part of their core curriculum. At most it is offered as an optional seminar or an additional workshop.

Until recently psychoanalytic training institutes refused to accept lesbian women or gay men for training – classical Freudian orthodoxy viewed their sexuality as a manifestation of 'unresolved and unanalysable neuroses'. It is still more difficult to gain a place on a psychotherapy training course if you are openly not heterosexual (Davies and Neal, 1996; 2000a) and those who are accepted frequently report a discomfort throughout the training, as much from the attitudes of their trainers and fellow trainees as from the heterosexist bias in the material being taught. Davies and Neal (1996) contend that there is institutionalized prejudice of a global nature operating in most British counsellor training programmes. Courses fail to attract students from all minorities and consequently fail to address the needs of clients from these groups. Course staff are often exclusively white, able-bodied heterosexuals; the course content and the majority of the students reflect the same bias.

What is significantly missing from training courses is both education about the experience of being homosexual and of living in a homophobic and heterosexist society, and any attempt to confront trainees with their own, inevitable prejudices and anti-homosexual attitudes. Without such input, our trained counsellors and therapists emerge with little self-awareness in this area and an inadequate ability to understand the specific needs and experiences of any gay or lesbian clients they may subsequently encounter. Furthermore, they will be largely unaware of their deficiency. As David Mair puts it: 'recognizing and owning homophobia and ignorance can be a threatening and painful process, and it appears that it is one which may often be sidestepped by both gay men and heterosexuals, clients and counsellors' (Mair, 2003: 33).

The seminal work for counselling and psychotherapy with gay and lesbian clients is widely recognised to be *Pink Therapy*, published by Davies and Neal in 1996; they followed this with *Therapeutic Perspectives on Working with Lesbian, Gay and Bisexual Clients* and *Issues in Therapy with Lesbian, Gay, Bisexual and Transgendered Clients* in 2000. Davies and Neal offer a model of 'gay affirmative therapy' whose emphasis is, as the name implies, affirmation of lesbian and gay identity as a positive human experience and expression equal to that of heterosexual identity. They emphasize that, because we have all been exposed to society's negative messages about homosexuality, therapeutic neutrality is impossible. Therapists, therefore, have a duty to explore their own values for attitudes that may cause them difficulty. An essential part of this is an understanding and acceptance, by therapists, of their own homosexual feelings as well as an awareness of the extent to which they have internalized society's homophobic attitudes. An understanding by the therapist of the kinds of experiences the gay or lesbian client will have encountered is an important part of helping the client confront any shame, guilt and internalized homophobia. There is a high probability of such clients feeling devalued and worthless internally, however successful they may appear outwardly, as a result of cultural discrimination against sexual difference.

The second volume of Davies and Neal's trilogy consists of a collection of contributions examining gay and lesbian therapy from a variety of different theoretical perspectives. The consensus that emerges from this, as from their other works, is that the therapist needs to have examined his or her own prejudices and sexuality deeply and thoroughly before embarking on this work. Furthermore, practitioners need considerable information and understanding about homophobia, homosexual experiences, and gay and lesbian life-styles. Some but not all contributors would argue that in this context the therapist should be willing to provide information and act as an educator, for example about the stages of coming out, the local lesbian and gay community, and HIV awareness.

Davies and Neal do not hold the view that it is essential for the sexual orientation of the therapist to be the same as the client. A heterosexual therapist can provide a positive experience by gaining the client's respect and thus helping to heal the wounds of heterosexism. If, however, the therapist is homosexual, he or she can act as a positive role model for the client. An alternative view is put by Young (1995) who believes that significant differences between client and therapist, be they of gender, sexual orientation, race or class, automatically cause problems in the relationship which will render the therapy ineffective. Young's view of effective therapy for lesbian clients tends towards a more radical position. She takes the stance that lesbians are rarely fully understood by therapists. This, she believes, is because lesbians, having intimate and painful experience of being a persecuted minority, have developed considerably more self-awareness, understanding and insight than most therapists, who are predominantly white, middle-class and heterosexual and who are consequently hampered in their ability to fully empathize with the issues and experiences being brought by their lesbian clients.

The issue of the need for a therapist to share, on a personal level, elements of a client's lived experience, is one which has been extensively debated in relation to sexuality, gender, race and many other factors. While it is clearly impossible to 'match' client and therapist in every element of personality and experience, the question remains as to whether it is desirable in specific instances where the disparity may be so great as to be obstructive for the client. In my view the element that is most likely to impede the psychotherapeutic relationship is a normative stance on the part of the therapist. Such a blinkered position is the result both of ignorance about other people's experiences and

SEXUALITY | **135**

world-views and a denial, by the practitioner, of his or her own internal biases. In regard to sexuality I see no reason why a therapist should not be able to work with a client whose sexual practices are different from his/her own, provided the therapist is aware of the issues of heterosexism and homophobia and has, as far as it is possible, thoroughly and honestly examined his/her own sexuality and prejudices. Theoretically, the client of course is always free to choose a counsellor or therapist whose sexuality is close to their own. There are increasing numbers of therapists and counsellors of all sexual orientations, despite the difficulties they are likely to encounter in achieving professional status. Their numbers, however, are still small, and they are by no means widespread throughout the country.

There are the beginnings, within the counselling and psychotherapeutic world, of a recognition that the lifestyles painfully constructed by gay men and lesbian women, and without social validation, may contain much from which heterosexuals could fruitfully learn. Traditional social models of family relationships are being challenged in many western societies. As Sketchley puts it: 'homosexual people have much to teach their heterosexual counterparts about personal commitment, rather than external pressures or sexual activity, serving as the basis for committed relationships' (Sketchley, 1989: 250). In many institutes and counselling centres gay men and lesbian women are now able to train and practise as counsellors and therapists, and to participate in the training of others. But the beginnings are small, and the process much too slow. Although there is no longer any direct bar to gay and lesbian people training as counsellors or psychotherapists, the legacy of the past may well deter many from even applying. The homophobic attitudes, which have pervaded our society for so long, are still very evident within the enterprises of counselling and psychotherapy. Davies and Neal (1996) catalogue the ways these can be seen in the counselling and therapy community – in training, supervision or general debate: joking about homosexuality, uneasiness, hostility or stereotyping, denial, exaggerating the significance of a client's sexual orientation, pity, and taking the view that sexual orientation makes no difference, thus ignoring the impact of anti-homosexual attitudes. In my own experience all of these responses are, sadly, familiar – I have encountered them among colleagues and students whom, in other respects, I would regard as people with integrity and insight.

As we have seen, the current counselling and psychotherapy trainings include scanty input regarding homosexuality, or even sexuality, and the prevailing ethos in the bulk of the material taught has a predominantly heterosexist bias. Counsellors and therapists emerge, however, with the belief that the skills and knowledge they have acquired will equip them to deal with any problems that their clients might bring. This is doomed to create a situation where clients who are not heterosexual feel marginalized, misunderstood or, worse, patronized. Small wonder that many feel the only therapeutic help that can really be effective for them is with therapists who share their experience of being part of a sexual minority.

Of all the issues covered in this book this is the one where I feel there is the greatest risk of practitioners *not* being aware of their own hidden prejudices, precisely because the element which is the focus of that prejudice is, to some extent, present in all of us. Sexuality is complex and diverse; its potentialities of expression transcend the socially imposed divisions and categories that were invented by the sexologists and, in large part, have survived to this day. The implicit social sanctions against challenging the boundaries of these divisions are strong and deeply embedded in our culture and its institutions. The homosexual or lesbian client embodies an element of our being which we have been socialized into disowning; for many practitioners, encountering this element in another is both disturbing and problematic.

5 | Mental Illness

THE TITLE OF THIS CHAPTER IS, in itself, controversial enough to have been the subject of academic discussions that have filled whole books. What is mental illness (or 'mental illness')? Does it really exist? Are we referring to something that is of the mind, of the brain, or of the whole person? Is it an illness? (What is an illness anyway?) Or is it a cluster of random symptoms and behaviours? Or one point on a wide continuum of possible human experiences? It is outside the scope of this book to discuss in depth the attempts that have been made to answer these and other related questions, though I will be touching on many of the relevant theories and hope that the bibliography will point the interested reader in the right direction for further study.

Numerous terms have been used to describe what is universally recognized to be a painful and profoundly disturbing experience: lunacy, madness, insanity, mental illness, psychological disturbance – with a plethora of subcategories such as 'catatonia', 'hysteria', 'paranoia', 'neurosis', 'psychosis', 'schizophrenia', 'manic-depression', 'melancholia', 'mania', and many more. The terminology that currently holds sway in the literature and in the forum of public discourse is the term 'mental disorder', or, where possible, the neutral 'mental health'. This is the legacy of political correctness – we can no longer say someone has 'gone mad', but must describe him or her as having 'mental health issues'. Such linguistic circumlocutions, however, do nothing to reduce the stigmatization and discrimination which have always been society's response to the mad.

The observation of strange symptoms or types of behaviour appears to generate the need to categorize or give this behaviour/condition a name, or diagnosis. It also leads to attempts to find both the cause of the condition and the solution, or best treatment. But diagnostic categories for mental disorders are notoriously arbitrary, shifting and changing over time. The two major current diagnostic classification systems, the DSM (*Diagnostic and Statistical Manual of Mental Disorders*, produced by the American Psychiatric Association) and the ICD (*International Classification of Diseases*, produced by the World Health Organization), have both undergone numerous changes and revisions, and do not even now agree in their descriptions of symptoms for many of the mental illnesses. A diagnosis very often carries with it implications concerning cause and treatment. It would be comforting to assume that the theory (or preferably knowledge) about the cause of a problem informs the diagnosis and treatment. Such an assumption cannot always be made. In looking at the status of those deemed mad, both now and historically, it would appear that in many instances the theory as to cause provides a *post hoc* justification of the treatment, without such theories necessarily having been proved to be correct. Furthermore, our knowledge in this area is far from complete. Innumerable hypotheses have been advanced concerning the aetiology, course and outcome of mental disorders, and innumerable methods of treatment have been implemented. Research and clinical practice have both failed to come up with any definitive answers. History appears to show that the explanation of mental disorders has always been controversial, with numerous ideas in circulation at any one time. This is a situation that continues today.

While it is clearly difficult to tease apart the different strands of aetiological theory, diagnosis and treatment, I will attempt to do so to some degree in this chapter by looking first at the history of madness, focusing mainly on the treatment that it has attracted – social, medical and otherwise. There follows a summary of the principal theories regarding the nature and cause of mental disturbances. The third section deals with the relationship between mental illness/health and psychotherapy and counselling. As the topic of mental illness appears to be a place where the other subjects of this book intersect, the final section of this chapter examines the complex and disturbing relationship between mental illness and the experience of being in another minority group. For being a lunatic, a madman or madwoman, a mental patient, or a person with a psychiatric diagnosis has the effect of rendering a person outside the norm, and as such the recipient of discriminatory attitudes and prejudice. In 1972 Manfred Bleuler urged us to see the mental patient as a 'fellow sufferer and comrade in arms' rather than someone whom 'a pathological heritage or a degenerate brain has rendered inaccessible, inhuman, different or strange' (Bleuler, 1972). It would appear his appeal has not yet been answered.

The treatment of madness – a historical overview

Madness has existed in all societies, past and present. The ways in which it has been interpreted and responded to have differed widely over time and place, treatment ranging from the benign to the abusive and cruel.

Early history

Archaeological evidence reveals the practice of trepanning – boring a hole in the skull, presumably to allow the release of devils – as early as 5000 BC (Porter, 2002). Beliefs about supernatural possession were common in the classical world, as evidenced by the wealth of literature from that period: the treatment for such conditions was prayers, incantations and sacrifices. From the fourth century BC the writings of Hippocrates (*c.* 460–377 BC) cast a different light on the concepts of health and sickness. He dismissed the idea of a diabolical cause for madness, or any other aspect of human behaviour, seeing all emotional experiences, including anxiety, delirium and madness as emanating from the brain. Hippocratic medicine explained all illness, mental and physical, in terms of the 'humours' – vital bodily fluids which, by their relative balance, determined the physiology, temperament and health of an individual. The four humours, blood, choler, phlegm and bile, were seen as being related to the four elements of the universe – air, fire, water and earth respectively. This system was holistic, viewing mental and physical conditions as extensions of each other. Treatment for madness was varied, the most common being blood-letting. Diet and exercise were also recommended, as was talking to the deranged person. Others advocated shock treatment and isolation in total darkness. Both Greek and Roman law attempted to regulate the insane, holding their families responsible for their containment. Even after humoral theories had gained ascendance, public belief in diabolical possession continued in the classical world and the deranged were generally feared and shunned. The medical tradition begun by Hippocrates, based on the humoral approach, continued through the medieval period and into the Renaissance.

The advent of Christianity saw a return to the idea of madness as caused by the devil, who was seen as locked in battle with God for possession of individual human souls. Insanity was deeply shameful and in early Christian Europe families frequently kept deranged individuals locked up. In the Islamic empire a similar approach led to the establishment of mental hospitals called *moristans* as early as the thirteenth century (Fernando, 2002: 72). By the end of the Middle Ages in Europe there was the beginning of a more formal segregation of the insane, religious institutions providing for their custody or care. St Mary's of Bethlehem, a religious house in London, was founded in 1247. It was catering for lunatics by the end of the fourteenth century and was later known as 'Bedlam'. Similar asylums were established throughout Europe by the fifteenth century, largely under religious jurisdiction. Treatment in these institutions included perforating the skull (for 'mania'), 'plaguing with squealing pigs', rest and quiet, punching and thrashing, binding with ropes, and exorcism (Howells, 1991: 34). In St Mary's of Bethlehem patients were kept chained to the wall or on long leashes, in cramped and unsanitary conditions. They were also exposed to public exhibition as freaks of nature. As early as 1324 in England, 'lunatics' lost their civil rights and their property was taken over by the crown (ibid.: 42).

In the late fifteenth century religious fervour caused unprecedented levels of persecution in the witch craze which spread across Europe. Symptoms of madness were attributed to satanic *maleficium* (malice) caused by witches who had compacted with the devil. Over 200,000 people, mostly women, were executed during this period. Religious doctrine justified this with a self-serving circular argument by which 'the mad were judged to be possessed, and religious adversaries were deemed out of their mind' (Porter, 2002: 21). In his seminal work *The Myth of Mental Illness* (1962), Thomas Szasz draws a parallel between the fate of witches in the Middle Ages and that of mental patients in the late twentieth century, seeing both as scapegoats for the society of their time. Others (for example, Sedgwick, 1982) are critical of Szasz's analogy, pointing out that the mentally ill were seen as evidence of witchcraft, rather than themselves being accused of it. Be that as it may, this lamentable episode in history is a chilling example of the treatment meted out to those seen as odd or different – the vulnerable, the deranged, those on the margins of society.

Philosophical developments in the seventeenth century had profound implications for the treatment of those deemed insane. Descartes' distinction between mind and matter (including the body) led to a conceptualization which conflated the mind with the soul, encompassing consciousness, moral responsibility, immortality and rationality. Treatment had to be aimed at the body, for to implicate the mind (or soul) in insanity would be to call into question the soul's immortality and hence the very foundations of Christianity. Thinking in this period held reason and rationality to be the one capacity that distinguished man from animals. Insanity was characterized as loss of reason, or as delusional thinking or faulty cognition. (The parallels with the theories underlying twentieth-century cognitive therapy are striking.) There was a belief then (as now) that the mentally disturbed could be re-trained to think correctly. However, the favoured method in the seventeenth century was the use of fear to restore reason. This gave a mandate for a variety of abusive physical treatments, justified on the basis that the insane were no longer human because they were without reason – so could be treated like animals (Scull, 1981; Seligman and Rosenhan, 1998).

Institutionalization – the eighteenth and nineteenth centuries

As societies became more organized it seemed to become more imperative to exclude the socially deviant from the social mainstream. The eighteenth century saw a steady rise in the number of institutions dedicated to the custody of the insane. Many of these were private institutions, the 'pauper lunatic' usually being assigned to the miseries of the workhouse. There was no regulation of such institutions until towards the end of the century, and no laws governing the criteria to justify incarceration in a 'madhouse'.

Foucault describes this Europe-wide institutionalization as the 'great confinement' of the mad and the poor, a movement of 'blind repression' (Foucault, 1965). Thus people were shut away not as a therapeutic measure but as a custodial act of state. Porter (2002) criticizes Foucault's interpretation as simplistic and over-generalized. The involvement of the state in the incarceration of the mad in the eighteenth and nineteenth centuries did indeed vary from country to country, as did the nature of the regimes within these institutions. Some were clearly worse than others, but all inmates were locked away, for indefinite periods of time, with no means of securing their own release. What emerges clearly, however, is that the medicalization of insanity came after the great era of asylum building. The original impetus for their construction came from religious organizations; the involvement of the state and the medical profession became apparent in the late eighteenth century, gaining ascendancy in most countries by the mid-nineteenth century. In England, Acts were passed in 1842 and 1845 which made the erection of county and borough asylums mandatory. By this time a medical presence in the asylums was also required.

The medical model and the rise of psychiatry
Medical theories about madness began to proliferate; insanity was characterized as a mental disorder, a pathology, and medical treatment within the asylums was vaunted as the means to restore the insane to health. The optimism of this era, which viewed lunacy as curable, generated for a brief period a humanitarian approach to the treatment of the insane – namely, 'moral therapy', which was a reaction against the chains, whippings, dungeons and other physical treatments to which asylum inmates had hitherto been subjected. Many hospitals began to remove restraints and unlock their wards. The Retreat in York, established in 1796, is often cited as the supreme example

of this new approach. The emphasis here was on community living, with kindness, consideration and dignity the values propounded as essential for the care of patients. Other relatively benign treatments practised in the eighteenth and nineteenth centuries included mesmerism and hypnotism, the latter pioneered by Jean Martin Charcot at La Salpêtrière in Paris. Charcot's methods were ultimately discredited but hypnotism continued to be practised widely in Europe and America well into the twentieth century. It has returned more recently in the form of hypnotherapy.

The era of moral therapy, however, was short-lived, and by the late nineteenth century most asylums had reverted to being closed, overcrowded institutions with rigid, harsh regimes and little chance of release for those committed to them. The explanations for this are legion. One argument is that the optimism about the curability of insanity proved to be unfounded, and that consequently numbers in the asylums rose and any attempt at benevolence became impractical as well as discredited as a form of treatment (Barham, 1992). Other commentators point to the rise in psychiatry as a medical speciality, and to the need for psychiatrists to justify their existence and their hold over the mad as their special area of concern, by establishing a physical basis for insanity. Moral therapy threatened this, so it had to go (Scull, 1981). An alternative explanation is that asylums became a form of social regulation – the place for those who were unwanted by society by dint of being odd, or mad, or poor, or socially deviant (Sedgwick, 1982). Whatever the reason, the effect on those classified as mad was one of punitive segregation and social ostracism. By the end of the nineteenth century the incurability of insanity was taken for granted, and the fast-growing asylum system had accentuated society's fears of the insane. Locking people up is an excellent way of conveying the message that those under lock and key are dangerous and unfit to be included in 'normal' society. It is no coincidence that the

Victorian madhouse keeper, or psychiatrist, was called an 'alienist', whose job was to identify and control those 'alienated' from society by virtue of their lack of sanity or rationality. As Roy Porter puts it, this was, in effect, a process of sanctioning 'the stigmatization and exclusion of "outsiders" and "aliens" … The walled and locked asylum … backed by the medical specialty of institutional psychiatry … underscored the differentness, the uniqueness, of those thus "alienated" or "excluded"' (Porter, 1987: 25).

The rise of psychiatry was based on the assumption that insanity had an organic aetiology. Research began into the pathology of the brain which was assumed by many to be the root of 'mental disease'. The concept of insanity as illness was given considerable credibility by the discovery in 1897 of the link between syphilis and paresis (insanity resulting, sometimes many years later, from syphilitic infection). This led to research into the biological foundations of all other mental disorders – research which continues to the present day. Some other conditions have been found to have a physical basis, but no such neat biological link has been found for the major 'mental illnesses' such as schizophrenia, manic depression or paranoia. Other theories which gained ground at the turn of the twentieth century concerned the possibility of inherited psychopathic tendencies. This so-called 'degenerationist' model suggested that such tendencies accumulated and worsened over generations – thinking which was given scientific support by the evolutionary ideas of the time. Degenerate traits were posited to be present in non-European races, in sexual 'inverts' (that is homosexuals) and in women. Degenerationist ideas were the 'scientific' foundations of eugenics. In America by 1900 there were calls for compulsory confinement and sterilization for those judged to be insane, or degenerate in other ways, as well as for the use of psychiatry in immigration control (Porter, 2002: 152). Psychiatric sterilization was widely practised in America and other

European countries well before the rise of Nazism in Germany. Degenerationism and eugenics reached their zenith in the killing of a quarter of a million mental patients by the Nazis between 1940 and 1942 – an act justified by the concept of 'life unworthy of life' (Barham, 1992: 79).

Twentieth-century approaches

The beginning of the twentieth century saw a significant split in the treatment of the mentally disturbed which persists to the present day. In simple terms the split is between somatic and psychological approaches. Freud's theories lent considerable weight to the psychological camp but it is significant that Freud, and many of his colleagues, worked mainly with the less seriously disturbed. Freudian thought created a division between the 'neurotic' and the 'psychotic', with the belief that paranoid and psychotic patients were unable to form a transference and were therefore unamenable to psychoanalysis. Some post-Freudians, and many psychotherapists from other schools, have used psychoanalysis and psychotherapy to treat schizophrenia, manic-depression and other mental illnesses, but the overarching distinction persists: therapy and counselling are for the 'worried well'; the insane remain the domain of the psychiatrists. As such they have been subjected to a wide variety of physical treatments. Shock treatments of various kinds have been used, at first with insulin therapy and then, by the 1940s, with ECT (electro-convulsive therapy). Prolonged-sleep therapy, induced by barbiturates, was practised for a time in the 1920s, and psychosurgery has been widely used since the 1930s. Many of these interventions had the effect of rendering patients placid and submissive. There is inevitably much controversy over the desirability of such an outcome. These treatments were invasive, unpleasant and very often carried out without the patient's consent. Many had permanent, and not necessarily beneficial, effects. Psychiatry, meanwhile, was gaining in credibility as a medical speciality. These developments can either be seen as the desperate attempts of well-meaning doctors to help the afflicted, or as the abuse of powerless patients used as guinea pigs by arrogant and power-hungry psychiatrists. The truth surely lies somewhere between these two extremes.

The 1950s saw the beginning of the drug revolution. Anti-depressant and anti-psychotic drugs came into use and rapidly became the favoured treatment for all kinds of mental disturbances. Extravagant claims have been made for the effectiveness of these drugs. At best they appear to reduce, or mask, symptoms such as anxiety, depression, hallucinations, paranoia, etc. Many people with debilitating conditions such as severe depression, mania and schizophrenia are able to manage their symptoms with medication in such a way as to lead relatively normal and fulfilling lives. However, they offer no cure and are only effective as long as they are being taken, their effectiveness often reducing over time. Most worryingly, the side-effects of these drugs are little publicized. In 1990 Pilgrim estimated that around half of the world's 150 million users of major tranquillizers suffered from tardive dyskinesia (Pilgrim, 1990: 228), a condition resulting from permanent damage to the central nervous system which causes involuntary and uncontrollable movements of the face, body and limbs. Peter Breggin identifies not only tardive dyskinesia but also tardive dementia, which he describes as 'a global deterioration of the mind and mental faculties caused by the [neuroleptic] drugs' (Breggin, 1993: 86). His investigation of clinical studies in the USA on tardive dyskinesia revealed that many and sometimes all patients in these studies were also suffering from serious mental dysfunction, including dementia, as a direct result of long-term use of psychotropic medication.

Many consider that the main purpose the psychotropic drugs serve is to render patients calm and manageable

(Sedgwick, 1982; Newnes, 1999). In the crowded mental institutions of the first half of the twentieth century this had obvious benefits. The stated purpose of such drugs is to relieve disturbing psychological and behavioural symptoms – symptoms which the biological theories claim are caused by biochemical imbalances in the brain or nervous system. However, there are some who maintain that the drugs pre-date the theories, which they say are a *post hoc* justification for drugging mental patients into submission (Newnes, 1999). While it is difficult to disentangle the exact sequence of events, it is indisputable that the biological theories clearly gave massive credibility to the use of these drugs. Scepticism is further fuelled by the fact that the drug companies themselves are the major source of funds for research in this field. Furthermore, research findings are compromised by the fact that patients studied in the attempt to demonstrate brain biochemical abnormality in those with a diagnosis such as manic-depression or schizophrenia will have already been treated with the neuroleptic drugs, substances known to cause brain damage. The therapeutic effectiveness of the anti-psychotic drugs has been seriously questioned by a number of studies. In a survey of such studies Scull (1984: 87) concludes that large doses function as a 'chemical straitjacket' and lower doses have little or no effect in comparison with a placebo.

The advent of drug therapy is often offered as the explanation for the de-institutionalization of mental patients which took place throughout Europe and in the USA around the middle of the last century. In fact this had already begun in most places before such drugs were widely available. In the UK the decline in the numbers of mental patients in hospital began in the early 1950s and continued steadily throughout the rest of the century. By the 1980s many mental hospitals had closed down. The pattern was similar in other European countries and was the result of specific governmental policy. A benevolent reading of such

policy would place at its centre a desire to reform the
outdated and repressive regimes of these Victorian institutions and replace them with a more humanitarian approach
to mental disorder. An indisputable outcome, intended or
not, was a massive cost saving. The facilities intended to
replace the care and treatment provided by the mental
hospitals were either slow in arriving or never appeared at
all. Many people who had been in hospital for extended
periods were ill-equipped to adjust to life outside an institution, and one of the direct results of de-institutionalization
has been an increase in the number and proportion of people with mental health problems among the homeless and in
prisons. Over the past thirty-five years in the UK, 100,000
long-stay patients have been discharged from psychiatric
hospitals but fewer than 4,000 places have been provided in
local authority hostels (Barham, 1992: 17). There is also a
growing number of so-called 'revolving-door' patients –
short-stay patients with frequent admissions.

The contemporary situation
The policy of 'Care in the Community' is generally recognized to be far from successful, partly due to a woeful lack
of resources, partly due, it seems, to a lack of political will,
and partly because, as a policy, it is inherently flawed. It is
based on an assumption that the community will *want* to
care for its less fortunate individuals – those deemed mentally ill. Sadly, this is far from being the case. Mental health
patients experience many practical problems to do with the
management of their daily lives, but on top of that they are
subjected to social isolation and exclusion as well as to a
dearth of services. As Richard Warner puts it: 'much of
what today is called community treatment, is, in fact, the
antithesis of treatment: people suffering from psychosis are
consigned to a sordid, impoverished existence in which even
basic needs, such as food and shelter, are not met' (Warner,
1994: x). There is a huge gulf between the aspirations of

social policy-makers who talk about maintaining vulnerable patients 'in an appropriate setting in their community, free to come and go and to participate in an urban environment' (Bennett and Morris, 1983) and the reality for most people with severe mental disorders. Such people are aware that disclosure of a psychiatric diagnosis will make it more or less impossible for them to obtain a job or decent housing. It will also work against them in any efforts at social integration. Their access to medical services is restricted to, at best, a monitoring of their medication, or, more usually, repetition of prescriptions without even a consultation with a doctor. Should they make the choice to discontinue taking their prescribed drugs, they are at risk of being compulsorily committed.

The process of involuntary admission to a psychiatric hospital is based on specific criteria, all of which are the result of subjective judgement, such judgement being delivered by a psychiatrist. The criteria are: the presence of a mental disorder, the judgement that absence of treatment would lead to deterioration in the person's mental state, and the belief that the person represents a serious danger to themselves or another person. These criteria are contained in the 1983 Mental Health Act which also gives professionals legal powers to override an individual's right to decline treatment on the basis that they, the professionals, know best. Patients committed involuntarily thus have few civil rights and their stay in hospital can be indefinitely extended on the recommendation of the psychiatrist. Under the current law, people can only be given treatment against their will if they are detained in hospital, although the 1996 Mental Health (Patients in the Community) Act provides for the compulsory *supervision* of patients in the community, and alongside that gives professionals the power to remove a patient to hospital (where they can be treated involuntarily) if the patient does not adhere to an agreed treatment plan. However, the proposed Mental

Health Act reforms contained in a draft bill published by the Department of Health in June 2002 includes the proposal to extend compulsory *treatment* to those outside hospital. This has caused grave concern in many quarters. A Mind Policy Briefing points out that Community Treatment Orders 'would either make users too frightened of the consequences to contact services or discourage them from seeking help. This cuts people off from the very services which should provide help and support, thus making a deterioration of their condition more likely' (Mind Policy Briefing, 2002a: 2). The situation is made worse by the fact that the structure of funding for resources in the UK is such that very often money granted for mental health care is used for areas where results are more easily seen, and the 'hopeless' cases – the long-term mentally ill – are frequently overlooked.

It is clear that the insane, the mad, the mentally ill, have been universally stigmatized throughout history. They arouse in others feelings of anxiety and fear. Bowers (1998: 128) suggests that this response is caused by several factors. Their perceived unpredictability makes us fearful for our own safety and the inexplicability of mental illness threatens our need for logic and reason. Furthermore, it reminds us of our own potential for madness, something we would prefer not to think of. Mental illness lessens the humanity of the sufferer and generates in others feelings of revulsion and a fear of contamination. This is essentially a process of dehumanization which sheds light on much of the inhumane treatment the mad have been subjected to over time. The stereotype of the unpredictable, potentially violent maniac is one which is particularly prevalent today. The current, and proposed, mental health laws are heavily skewed towards measures to protect the public from these lunatics, rather than measures to enable the latter to recover their sanity. Mind's Policy Briefing (2002a) quotes an article in the *British Journal of Psychiatry* which showed that between 1957 and 1995 in the UK there was overall a fivefold increase in homicide, but in the same period a 3 per cent decline per annum in the contribution to these figures by people with mental illnesses. Despite this, 'two-thirds of media reports misleadingly portray people with mental health problems as violent' (Mind Policy Briefing, 2002b: 1).

The split between psychological and physical treatments still prevails. On the whole, the worse your condition is judged to be, the more likely you are to be given a physical treatment – usually drug therapy. A growing sense of unease about the efficacy of such treatments, combined with a resistance to the infringement of civil liberties implicated in many psychiatric interventions, has given rise to the service user/survivor movement. Begun in the 1980s, this movement is at heart a reaction by its members to being seen in terms of a diagnosis, and a challenge to the discrimination and marginalization that they experience as a result of the perceived status of the diagnosed mentally ill in society. There is a powerful argument that much of the prejudice against the mentally ill is *created* by the disease model, with its battery of psychiatric diagnoses and labels. I will be examining the concept of the disease model in the next section. It is disquieting to note, however, that the concept of mental disturbance as an illness, with its assumption of a physical cause and concomitant physical treatment, appears to be getting ever wider and all-encompassing.

All kinds of human behaviour have now been given a psychiatric diagnostic label which, by definition, carries with it implications that this should/could be treated. Some of the more recent 'discoveries' have been 'attention deficit hyperactivity disorder' (ADHD), 'pre-menstrual dysphoric disorder', 'gender identity disorder' and the worryingly catch-all 'personality disorder'. The diagnosis of 'personality disorder' has the effect of drastically reducing the services on offer to those to whom it is applied. As it is considered to be unamenable to treatment, appointments with a CPN or even a psychiatrist are withdrawn. The individual with a 'personality disorder' is left on a prescribed drug regime infrequently monitored by his/her GP. The idea of a physical cause for all illnesses, including those considered mental, has been further fuelled by the Genome Project. Many assume that before too long the genes for all illnesses and disorders will be identified and we will then be in a position to 'engineer' them out of existence. This prospect raises a number of ethical questions, not the least of which centres on the definition of what exactly *is* a mental illness, which is where we came in!

Theories about mental illness

As we have seen in the previous section, by the end of the nineteenth century there was general acceptance that certain behavioural patterns and mental states were the result of illness, rather than the consequence of possession by demons or a state of sin. This brought madness out of the jurisdiction of religion into that of medical science. Parallel with this development was the growing acceptance that the mind is the function of brain. This belief gave rise to somatic psychiatry. In the early part of the twentieth century the development of psychology and, at that time more specifically psychoanalysis, led to a break between physical and psychological modes of treatment. The central issues in these developments – the status of mental illness and the relationship of mental functioning to brain anatomy and physiology – remain with us, and are still unresolved. Much of the literature on this subject takes the form of impassioned attacks on the discipline of psychiatry, which, by definition, embraces the medical model.

The medical model
This is the model of madness which has general public acceptance. Any newspaper account, or radio or TV item

on the subject is based on the premise that madness in any of its manifestations has a physical basis and consequently should receive medical attention. This is doubtless partly due to our cultural faith in science and our belief that we should, by right, be in full possession of physical and mental health at all times. Should this not be the case, we believe or hope that a pill will put it right. Since the discovery of the link between paresis and syphilis in 1897, and the invention of penicillin and antibiotics, people have been searching for a similar biological basis for all other mental disorders. Other conditions have indeed been established as having a physical origin: Alzheimer's, Wernicke's encephalopathy, Korsakoff psychosis, alcohol-induced psychosis, and the like.

The focus on an organic basis for mental disorder has gained further credibility with research in the neural sciences, which appears to provide evidence for measurable physical disturbances and differences in people with specific disorders. An example of this is the predominant biochemical theory of schizophrenia – the dopamine hypothesis – which suggests that the underlying abnormality may be a relative overactivity of tracts of neurons in which dopamine is the chemical mediator (Warner, 1994: 18). Other research has identified degenerative changes in the limbic system area of the brain in schizophrenic patients. This is not present in all schizophrenics, but it is important to note that it has been found not only in those patients who have been treated with neuroleptic drugs but also in those who have not (ibid.). The degree of influence of genetic characteristics on the emergence and pattern of mental disorders is highly debated. Much research in this area appears to point to a genetic predisposition in disorders such as manic-depression and schizophrenia, rather than genetic factors being the total cause. Work by epidemiologist Irving Gottesman, drawing data from over forty European studies conducted between 1920 and 1987, reveals that the closer the relationship a person has to someone diagnosed with schizophrenia, the greater is the risk that that person may also develop the disorder. Thus, the identical twin of a schizophrenic, who has precisely the same genetic constitution, has a 50-per-cent risk, the rate in the general population being 1 per cent (Gottesman, 1991). Other studies focusing on twins who have been adopted or reared separately have produced concordance rates as high as 80 per cent in monozygotic (identical) twins for the manic-depressive disorders (Prior, 1999: 66). However, it is clear that genetics cannot be the whole story, as in all of these studies a significant proportion of the monozygotic twins did not develop the disorders. Moreover, nearly two-thirds of schizophrenic people have no relative at all with the illness (Warner, 1994: 21).

Research into the biology of depression has identified several physiological changes which are absent in the brains of people who are not depressed, for example platelet and lymphocyte 5HT binding site density, cation transport and cortisol secretion (Cowen and Wood, 1991). In all this research, however, there is an inherent danger of reductionism, and of reverting to a Cartesian split between mind and body. We know that the social, the psychological and the physiological intricately interact with each other. Stressful, and joyful, events have an impact on our physiology, just as physical illness affects our psychological state. It is a circular, chicken-and-egg process rather than a linear one of A causes B. A further cautionary note is struck by Len Bowers who points out that, for mental states, normality is not determined by structure or process in the brain, but by function, 'and with the brain, function will always have entirely social and psychological criteria'. He goes on:

It is the symptoms that are the criteria for deciding normality/health, and these are always psychosocial with mental illness. Otherwise I could say that having less than average intelligence was abnormal and an illness and perhaps be able to point to a discernible difference in brain function. Difference or variation in brain activity does not by itself equal malfunction. (Bowers, 1998: 175)

To date it would appear that physiological accounts of cause in mental illness are always partial, though this does not rule out the possibility that future research will discover something new in this area. The relationship between physiology and psychology is more complex than many of the theories within the medical model, together with the treatments that such theories legitimize, take into account.

Socio-cultural models
In the 1960s and 1970s a variety of theories emerged, all having as their base starting-point a rejection of the exclusively biological, physiological and genetic theories and an opposition to the traditional psychiatric theory and practice embodied in the medical model. The most vehement rejection of the medical model is manifested in a movement which has become known as anti-psychiatry. Its main proponents are generally accepted to be Thomas Szasz in the United States and R.D. Laing in the UK, although Szasz, in his book *Schizophrenia: The Sacred Symbol of Psychiatry* (1976), dissociated himself from the anti-psychiatry movement, claiming it to be as demeaning to the 'patient' as traditional psychiatry. Szasz's earlier book *The Myth of Mental Illness* (1962) dismisses the notion that mental disturbance of any kind is an 'illness' or a 'disease'. He views it rather as one way of surviving in a particular social situation. His perspective is broadly socio-political, seeing the mental patient as a scapegoat for society, made necessary by the discrepancy between prescribed rules of conduct and actual social behaviour. Consequently the more we insist on the axiom of psychological health and a balanced mental state, ignoring any other aspects of our personality, the greater our need to victimize those exhibiting psychological

disturbance. People so doing become 'sacrifices as a means of maintaining the social myth that man lives according to his officially declared ethical beliefs' (Szasz, 1962: 193). The notion of 'mental illness' is thus a rationalization for forms of social control dressed up in the guise of medical treatment, and the mental patient is the latest representation of 'the perennial scapegoat principle', replacing the witch, the Jew and the black slave in a long line of persecution and subjugation of non-conformity (Szasz, 1970; 2002).

R.D. Laing's work aims to demonstrate the meaningfulness and intelligibility of behaviour which has been labelled mad (usually schizophrenic). He progresses from seeing schizophrenia as a social and family creation, to a celebration of madness as one stage in a natural psychic healing process. In this light psychosis is viewed as a mystical experience, a journey towards primeval one-ness, a higher form of sanity (Laing, 1967). He eschewed drug therapy and established therapeutic communities for those diagnosed as mad.

The notion of social control is extended in the labelling theory of deviant behaviour. By diagnosing (or 'labelling') people as schizophrenic, manic-depressive, paranoid, and so forth, psychiatry is viewed as an instrument by which the status quo is maintained and deviants are marginalized – it becomes 'modern capitalism's ultimate weapon of social control against dissidence' (Sedgwick, 1982: 5). Labelling theory was first expounded by Howard Becker who proposed that 'social groups create deviance by making the rules whose infraction constitute deviance, and by applying those rules to particular people and labelling them as outsiders' (Becker, 1963: 9). Thus deviance 'is *not* a quality of the act' (ibid.) but a consequence of the labelling by someone observing and judging the act. The observation of behaviour, and categorization of that behaviour as deviant, produces a crucial change in self-identity within the person being labelled. From this the theory claims that 'labelling is the single most important cause of chronic mental illness' (Cochrane, 1983: 151).

Several studies have shown that the manifestation of behaviour which is taken as indicative of mental illness leads to social rejection, the likelihood of rejection being greater the more severe the disturbance adduced. Similarly, the experience of many who have acquired a psychiatric diagnosis is that disclosure of that diagnosis is likely to provoke similar levels of social rejection, even if their behaviour is manifestly symptom-free. Moreover, the theory suggests that the label itself, together with the attitudes and reactions of those who apply it, will produce such symptoms in the person being labelled. It is primarily in the mental hospitals that the identity transformation posited by this theory takes place, as so graphically described by Goffman in his book *Asylums* (1961), in which he suggests that the mental hospital is not a place of refuge and recovery, but an institutionalized form of repression and social conformity. Whereas the mental hospitals of the 1960s no longer exist, psychiatric labelling is alive and well, and inventing new diagnoses by the day. The stigmatization that it creates is very real, and a psychiatric diagnosis, unlike a bout of 'flu or a broken leg, does not fade with time.

Broader sociological approaches take the view that the factors most implicated in the incidence of psychological illness are nothing to do with biological or physiological abnormality and everything to do with such things as low social status, limited economic opportunity, unemployment, lack of social support and stressful life events. Furthermore, studies have shown a higher incidence of mental disorders of all kinds among women, the lower social classes and certain ethnic groups. Many of the arguments here fall again into the circular category. Studies have shown that lower social status is associated with a higher risk of psychological problems. The suggestion is, therefore, that these mental disorders are 'caused' by poor environment, lower educational value, excess of stress, and so on. However, an alternative explanation is the 'social drift' hypothesis which posits that those suffering from mental disorders will be less likely to maintain their educational status, job or profession, and will sink to the lowest socio-economic condition. A similar difficulty exists with an established correlation between depression and stressful life events. Do the stressful events cause the depression, or is it that people with 'disturbed personalities' are more likely to create disruptive life events? Cochrane (1983) provides a detailed review of this approach, and, while conceding that with many social factors no direct causal relationship with mental disorders can be definitively established, concludes that a combination of negative factors, such as poverty, lack of social support, membership of a social or racial minority group, and stressful life events can produce 'long-term and unrelieved mental arousal [which] may lead to psychological problems like neurotic anxiety, alcoholism, depression and possibly psychoses' (Cochrane, 1983: 113).

The argument for the social creation of mental disorders is taken further by others (for example, Warner, 1994; Barham, 1997). Warner argues that the attitudes of mental health professionals towards the mental patient are even more rejecting and dehumanizing than those of the general public. He cites an article by G. Serban published in 1979 in the *American Journal of Psychiatry* in which it was demonstrated that people with schizophrenia are capable of experiencing human emotions such as depression. The authors conclude that 'chronic schizophrenics do become depressed when they are aware of their marginal lifestyle in the community'. Warner asks, 'how could the editors of the Journal possibly imagine that such findings were worth publishing? Only by assuming that a number of their readers would have doubts about the human qualities of their schizophrenic patients' (Warner, 1994: 181). Warner then goes on to argue that the symptoms which are taken by psychiatrists as evidence of the illness (in this case schizophrenia) – depression, apathy, irritability, negativity, emotional over-dependence, social withdrawal, isolation and loneliness, loss of self-respect and a sense of time – are in fact socially induced and 'may be attributed to the purposeless lifestyle and second-class citizenship of the schizophrenic' (ibid.). It should be noted here that Warner fails to include the more florid symptoms associated with schizophrenia in his list. Nevertheless, his findings would appear to demonstrate that recovery from schizophrenia is most common in those who reject the 'mentally ill' identity and all the negative symptoms that mental professionals associate with it. This is made extremely difficult by a view (in western cultures) of schizophrenia and other 'mental illnesses' as chronic biological disorders from which a patient is never cured – in such a formulation a person who appears well is 'in remission' and thus is expected to become 'ill' again at any time.

In all these theories mental illness is seen as intricately related to the social environment of the individual. Some assert a social aetiology for mental disorders, some a high degree of influence by social forces and others that mental illness is thoroughly and completely socially constructed. The latter is demonstrated dramatically by the political abuses of psychiatry in the Soviet Union, where political dissidents were labelled insane and incarcerated in mental institutions or worse. It can also be seen in the ever-fluctuating diagnostic categories of the ICD and DSM, the most controversial of which was the decision by the American Psychiatric Association in 1973 to declassify homosexuality as an 'illness'.

Psychosocial and psychological models

Psychological theories for mental disturbance have existed throughout time. In the second century AD Galen posited that hysteria had a sexual basis; although he linked it to a physical malfunction of the uterus (*hystera*), he emphasized the psychological component of the disturbance. It was, of course, Freud, with his systematic formulations concerning the psychological nature of human distress, who had the biggest impact in this sphere. The concepts of the unconscious, repression and the potentially traumatic effects of early childhood experiences on later life have had a lasting influence on western psychological thought.

The psychoanalytic movement in its development not only as a therapy but also as a universal psychology tended to look at the less serious 'neurotic' disorders. However, there have always been exceptions to this. In 1911 Eugen Bleuler invented the term 'schizophrenia' and deployed psychoanalytic theory in his description of this condition. He saw it as a global splitting of mental functions, characterized by delusions, hallucinations, disordered thought and inappropriate affect. He felt that people with this condition were 'incapable of empathy, sinister and frightening' (Porter, 2002: 185); their outcome was poor and psychoanalysis ineffective. Jung also worked with the severely disturbed and reported some psychotherapeutic success (Jung, 1939), but the medical opinion at that time was that if a 'schizophrenic' patient recovered with therapy or analysis, then he/she was not suffering from schizophrenia.

Within psychoanalytic thought, the theories of the interpersonal school focus most on the more severely disturbed – the psychotic. A variety of formulations is offered. Psychosis is seen by several theorists as provoked by a defence against homosexual impulses, creating a regression to a primitive stage of narcissism; by others as a disturbance in the relationship between the ego and the outer world; and by yet others as a diminished ability to neutralize aggression. A defective super-ego is suggested, a fixation at the oral-sadistic stage of psychosexual development, or a rupture of the ego boundary leading to the creation of a false reality (Stone, 1991). Harry Stack Sullivan was most influential in working with psychotic patients. He saw schizophrenia as 'a disorder which is determined by the previous experience of the individual' (Sullivan, 1924: 12). The interpersonal relations to which the individual is exposed produce a defence reaction – an irrational 'unconscious' protection of the self. The defence may be against either external or internal stimuli, and leads the individual to psychotic excitements, substitutive rituals, transference of guilt to others, or total incapacitation. Sullivan writes: 'the mental structure is disassociated in such a fashion that the disintegrated portions regress in function to earlier levels of mental ontology, without parallelism in individual depth of regression' (ibid.: 13). There is then an eruption of primitive functions and a profound alteration of the egoistic structures.

A wider focus is offered by the family theorists, who attempt to explain the eruption of psychosis by examining the interpersonal relationships within an individual's immediate family context. Bateson et al.'s seminal paper 'Toward a Theory of Schizophrenia' (1956) proposed the mechanism of the 'double-bind' as being instrumental in the development of schizophrenic symptoms. In this mechanism one individual (the child) receives two conflicting messages from another (the parent, usually the mother) together with an injunction against commenting on the conflict or leaving the field. The child is thus in a 'no-win' situation where whatever he or she does will be construed as wrong, and therefore punishable. Bateson et al. stress that the pathogenic element arises from the constant and repetitive nature of the double bind, producing a person who is unskilled on all levels of expressing and receiving communication. Other authors have suggested similar pathogenic interactional patterns within the family. Haley (1967) described the 'perverse triangle' in which two individuals within a family form a covert coalition against a third person. As with the double bind the coalition is denied at a metacommunicative level. With these and other proposed mechanisms – fragmentation, mystification, transactional disqualification – the family is seen as a complex system of idiosyncratic rules, norms and modes of behaviour, where communication becomes fraught with conflict and double meaning. The more 'disturbed' the family, the more highly organized and restrictive the rules and patterns. In this context the 'psychotic' individual's behaviour is adaptive – symptomatic not of an individual 'sickness' but of the dysfunctional nature of his or her interpersonal environment.

Psychological theories for severe mental disturbance have had limited impact on the medical model. Their use within traditional psychiatry is negligible, despite the fact that many attempts have been made to offer psychoanalysis and psychotherapy to those judged insane, as we shall see in the next section.

In evaluating the plethora of theories regarding mental illness, disturbance, disorder, insanity, madness, or whatever it is called, what emerges is the subjective nature of the distinction between normality and abnormality, sanity and insanity. Such judgements have always been not only subjective but also dependent on a variety of socio-politico-economic variables which fluctuate over time and from place to place.

If 'society' is making these judgements, the whole decision-making process around who is sane and who is insane becomes a socio-political one. To be considered sane means to be viewed as conforming to the expectations and regulations of society and its norms. This fails to address the question of whether the expectations and values of a particular society are indeed right, just or humane. The distinction between social maladjustment or deviant behaviour and fully functioning mental and psychological capacity then becomes blurred. Being diagnosed insane may be an indication of deviance rather than of psychological or mental ill health. In this context psychiatry, psychotherapy and counselling all become potential instruments of social control – persuading, cajoling or forcing people back into compliance with a particular social role or position.

The danger is that if we travel too far down this line of thought we can lose sight of the reality of the suffering that goes with madness. The view of the mentally ill as misjudged visionaries with a better understanding of reality than us blinkered drones can also be misleading. To be with a person who is experiencing deep depression, or manic hyperactivity, or madness in any of its manifestations, is to witness someone in the grip of terrifying pain, distress and confusion. It is not a state that the individual welcomes, or would choose to perpetuate.

Mental illness and counselling and psychotherapy

As we have seen, psychological theory from Freud onwards has proposed a neat division of mental states into the neurotic and the psychotic – with the nebulous 'borderline disorders' hovering somewhere between the two. The barrier between neurosis and psychosis (or 'normal anxiety' and 'madness') is shored up by the way we view the two states, and the kinds of treatment they receive. This serves to reinforce the deception we perpetrate upon ourselves of believing that we are 'normal' (or perhaps at times a touch neurotic) and, as such, safe from lapsing into psychosis.

The division between neurosis and psychosis is underpinned by, and in its turn feeds into, our own fear of mental illness. It is a way of consigning those whose behaviour may remind us of our own (if unacknowledged) potential for madness to the category of 'other' – that is to say 'not us'. So, on the whole, the neurotic receive counselling and psychotherapy and the psychotic get drug treatment, ECT, hospitalization, and the like. Psychotherapy and counselling require an intimate personal encounter between two people over a period of time, sometimes prolonged. The administration of drugs and other physical treatments does not involve a close relationship between the person receiving the treatment and the person meting it out. Perhaps this is because such a relationship would be too frightening, too threatening for the professional, rather than because it would be of no benefit for the individual in distress.

If, on the other hand, we view mental health as a continuum which includes all forms of disturbance, from the mild to the most severe, then the possibility of having a creative interpersonal therapeutic relationship with someone who is severely disturbed becomes a possibility. By empathizing with and attempting to understand the nature of the experience of madness, we perforce touch on the ways in which such an experience is familiar to us, and the extent to which the 'other' (mad person) is similar to ourselves. This view has been expounded by Bertram Karon, who points out that despite the fact that psychological treatments have been demonstrated to be effective with schizophrenics, they are still largely avoided. He maintains that this is due to the fact that psychotherapy involves understanding the patient, and 'understanding schizophrenic persons means facing facts about ourselves, our families and our society that we do not want to know' (Karon, 1992: 192). The fear of psychosis is certainly endemic within the professions of psychotherapy and counselling just as much as in the wider social sphere. In my own experience of teaching and supervising counsellors, the suggestion of working with a client who may be mentally ill, or even one who has a history of mental illness, engenders almost universal panic and fear – a reaction which cannot be wholly explained by the counsellor's self-perceived lack of knowledge and experience. There is an assumption that this kind of work would be qualitatively different – based on the neurotic/psychotic split that all counsellors are familiar with. But there is also,

I believe, a fear of the insane which we all share. It is an almost visceral response which can arouse feelings of revulsion and an instinct to withdraw. As the accepting non-judgemental professionals we believe ourselves to be, we may have difficulty in acknowledging such responses. There is no doubt that we can be reminded of the fragile nature of our own sanity by an encounter with another's madness. Most people would prefer to avoid such reminders – the dread of disintegrating into insanity is many people's worst nightmare.

Psychotherapy with mental illness

Psychoanalysts who have advocated applying psycho-analytic and psychotherapeutic techniques to the severe mental disorders range from Harry Stack Sullivan and Frieda Fromm-Reichmann in the earlier part of the last century through to Bertram Karon and Gary VandenBos and many other contemporary practitioners. Freud commented in the *Introductory Lectures on Psychoanalysis* (1916–17) to the effect that psychotics cannot form transference relationships, hence psychoanalysis with them was of little use. Whereas some would argue that Freud's statements should be understood in the context in which they were made, and that privately he felt much progress could be achieved with psychotics, there is no doubt that his views, stated publicly, have acted as a deterrent to many generations of psychoanalysts and psychotherapists of all persuasions. Fromm-Reichmann specifically rejected this notion and, like Sullivan, worked extensively with schizophrenics and other psychotic patients. She explicitly eschewed the fundamental components of classical psychoanalytic procedure in working with psychotic patients: the couch, free association, interpretation, the detached impersonal attitude of the analyst, the assumption that all repressed content is of a sexual or hostile nature, the prohibition of 'acting out', the pretence that the analyst's values do not influence the therapy. What she advocated in place of all this was alertness and spontaneity, attention to the patient's own interpretations and meanings, awareness by the analyst of his own values, and the ability to convey convincingly his interest in the patient's growth (Fromm-Reichmann, 1943). The latter description will no doubt sound familiar to the modern student or practitioner of counselling or psychotherapy.

The concept of providing space for psychosis to be expressed and explored was put into practice most fully by R.D. Laing, David Cooper, Joseph Berke and their colleagues in the 1960s and 1970s. Laing's first therapeutic community, Kingsley Hall, was set up in 1965 by the Philadelphia Association, which by 1974 had established seven similar communities in London. In these residential centres individuals were allowed to give psychosis free rein, to explore and re-evaluate the meaning of their experiences, and were given no treatment they did not want. Laing described the process that people went through in his households as 'a natural sequence of experiences' (Laing, 1967: 102), likening it to death and rebirth, from which people emerge reintegrated at a higher level of functioning than before. He saw psychotic 'symptoms' not as indicative of illness or disintegration but as the beginning of the process of becoming well. It was crucial, therefore, that people be allowed to express and experience those 'symptoms' rather than have them 'treated' by drug therapy. Laing's methods met with fierce opposition from traditional psychiatry at the time, and have continued to be viewed as controversial by many.

Many other attempts have been made to treat psychotic disorders with psychotherapy. In the USA the Agnews Project in the 1970s demonstrated the non-therapeutic effects of medication on hospitalized schizophrenic patients, and was followed up by the founding of Diabasis, a residential centre for the treatment of psychosis with psychotherapy and without medication. Although short-lived, this project reported an 85 per cent success rate (Perry, 1972). It should be noted, however, that this result seems to focus on early improvement, no mention being made of long-term follow-up. Another experiment was conducted by Mosher and Menn – the Soteria House programme, set up in the 1970s. Also drug-free, this facility was largely informed by Laing's work and aimed at creating a cohesive group setting where regression was acceptable and possible. Comparisons were made at various stages with the progress of schizophrenic patients receiving traditional psychiatric treatment – neuroleptic drugs. The outcome for the drug-free patients compared very favourably with those who had received anti-psychotic medication, the former in some cases doing significantly better. Mosher and Menn conclude: 'our data indicate that antipsychotic drugs need not be used routinely with newly admitted schizophrenics if a nurturant, supportive psychosocial environment can be supplied in their stead' (Mosher and Menn, 1978).

Meanwhile Theodore Lidz, working and writing in the 1970s, was advocating the family therapy approach to schizophrenia in particular. Building on the work of Bateson and others, described earlier, he maintained that psychotherapy was entirely possible with schizophrenics and that it was unnecessary to look for biological or genetic causes; this disorder was totally comprehensible in terms of personality development, family interactions and the environment in which the individuals grew up (Lidz, 1975).

Karon and VandenBos (1981) provide a review and critique of the major studies which have attempted to assess the effectiveness of psychotherapy with schizophrenic patients. What emerges from this is that where the findings appeared to demonstrate that psychotherapy was ineffective, the therapists employed were either inexperienced overall, or inexperienced in working with psychotic individuals.

Furthermore, the belief of these therapists in the possibility of the efficacy of psychotherapy was, in many cases, questionable. The Michigan State Project (1966) attempted to overcome these difficulties by utilizing therapists experienced in dealing with severe psychological disturbance, with appropriate supervision. The results of the project demonstrated that 'psychotherapy produces significantly greater patient change than medication', that 'in the long run, psychotherapy costs less than treatment by medication', and that 'it is a good thing for the therapist to be experienced and to believe in the treatment he or she practises' (Karon and VandenBos, 1981: 453). Over and over again in the literature on this subject emphasis is laid on the importance of the relationship between the therapist and the client, Fromm-Reichmann going as far as to say that if a workable doctor–patient relationship seems impossible with a psychotic individual, 'it is due to the doctor's personality-difficulties, not to the patient's psychopathology' (Fromm-Reichmann, 1952: 91). These experienced practitioners tell us that it *is* possible to do psychotherapy with those who have a diagnosis of 'mental illness' – that there is meaning in the behaviour and symptomatology of such clients – and that with skilled therapeutic help these people can make sense of their world.

The current status of therapy and counselling for the mentally ill

Despite the evidence that treatments other than orthodox psychiatry can be very effective in working with severe mental disturbances, attempts to offer anything that departs from the interventions dictated by the prevailing ideologies of the time – the straitjacket, the asylum, electro-convulsive therapy or neuroleptic drugs – are like oases in a vast desert. They have had little impact on medical orthodoxy.

Through the medicalization of mental disorders, and, as we have seen, through the split in psychological theory between neurosis and psychosis, a division has been created between those disorders which are considered amenable to counselling and psychotherapy, and those which are not. There is an almost universal assumption that the more severe disturbances are outside the remit of the 'talking therapies' and come under the jurisdiction of the medical profession. The treatment of choice is usually drug therapy. This has had the effect of accentuating the undesirability of falling within the category of the 'mentally ill'. In some countries (the USA in particular) it is considered almost fashionable to be 'in therapy'. This is viewed by many as indicative of psychological health and a high degree of self-awareness. In the UK, being a recipient of counselling or therapy is still seen by some as somewhat suspect, though this is slowly changing. In all western cultures, however, the response to those who are diagnosed with a severe mental disturbance or mental illness or who are undergoing psychiatric treatment is one of suspicion, fear, incomprehension and 'otherness'. This has a profound impact not only on the social response such people receive, but on their prospects of establishing themselves in society in terms of appropriate education, employment, housing or social integration.

Within the state-run facilities in the UK, the provisions for the severely disturbed are significantly under-funded at all levels. Clinical psychologists have taken little interest in the mad, compared with less disturbed clinical populations. As Pilgrim puts it, they 'have sought to make a bid for legitimacy to manage the "neurotic" population, leaving madness to the medical profession' (Pilgrim, 1990: 223). Research into madness and its treatment has always had a biological slant, with psychotherapeutic approaches being largely neglected. This is hardly surprising, since most of the research money has been either supplied by drug companies or, when research is state-funded, regulated by committees dominated by psychiatrists. Both of these groups have a vested interest in further legitimizing traditional concepts as to the possible causes and treatment of the mental illnesses.

Many psychiatrists are fearful of working with drug-free patients. Having drugged them, however, the treatment that is offered usually consists of little more than a short consultation on a sporadic basis, the main purpose of which is to monitor the progress of the medication. Paradoxically, and ironically, many counsellors and psychotherapists are disinclined to see clients who are on medication. This in effect places the severely disturbed in a position where the *only* treatment open to them is drugs. Even if they are strong-minded and well-informed enough to refuse medication and attempt to access a counselling or psychotherapy service, the likelihood is that they will be turned away if they reveal 'psychotic' symptoms such as hallucinations, hearing voices or paranoid thought processes. The counselling and psychotherapy that is available in this country through the National Health Service or Social Service Departments can only be accessed through GPs and psychiatrists. It is limited and will almost certainly involve some degree of drug therapy. The many excellent counselling services operating throughout the country perpetuate the distinction between the 'worried well' and the 'mad'. Very few of them will accept clients with severe disturbances or a mental health history. Private psychotherapists and counsellors, while more often catering for such clients, are by definition only available to those who can pay for such treatment. As many studies have shown, one of the more immediate effects of experiencing severe mental disturbance is to reduce the individual to the lowest socio-economic status.

It is hardly surprising, therefore, that the 'mentally ill' avoid, if at all possible, admitting to a mental health problem. Diagnostic labelling will stigmatize them permanently, reducing their chances of social rehabilitation; psychiatric treatment is seen as unhelpful and potentially damaging;

and psychotherapy and counselling are by and large unavailable to them.

Mental illness and other minority groups

Social inequality can be seen in terms of dimensions of being, like gender, race, class, age and sexuality, which are 'hierarchies of domination that limit and restrict some people while privileging others' (Williams, 1999: 29). These hierarchies are centred on power relationships which benefit one group at the expense of another. Thus the differences between social groups are not simply about differences in life-style or cultural beliefs, but about fundamental inequalities based on the exercise of power. Psychiatry has been accused of abusing its power by removing or alienating social undesirables from the mainstream by virtue of diagnosing them as mentally ill. Whereas there are undoubtedly historical instances when this has been a conscious process, it is by no means the stated or implicit aim of modern psychiatry. Despite this, many would claim that the outcome, intended or not, of psychiatric treatment is often exactly that – the ostracism and social alienation of those diagnosed with a mental illness.

There are, however, other ways in which the relationship between mental illness and socially marginalized groups is problematic. The theories that underpin the most widely accepted forms of treatment for mental illness pay little attention to the existence of structural inequalities in our society. Attempts to explain the relationship between gender, race, sexuality or social class and mental health/illness very often focus on the individual's pathology rather than the experience of being part of a persecuted or repressed minority. And yet studies have shown that mental illness is more common in the socially disadvantaged groups (Cochrane, 1983). What emerges, therefore, is a situation where those people who are already a minority group and subject to discrimination and disadvantage, are more susceptible to succumbing to forms of mental or psychological distress which will place them at further risk of stigmatization and alienation – and this by virtue of their original 'out' status. As Williams states unequivocally, there is 'little doubt that social inequalities – including those based on gender, race and class – are a root cause of the despair, distress and confusion that is named "mental illness"' (Williams, 1999: 29). Discrimination is thus seen as a direct cause of mental illness. Another dimension to this process is that the very experience of being discriminated against can make someone behave in ways that are perceived by others (the dominant group) as strange, different, or even 'mentally ill' (Littlewood and Lipsedge, 1989). In other words, the responses that people may have to oppression are interpreted incorrectly as signs of mental disturbance. Diagnosis and 'treatment' are then a way of diverting attention from the inequalities and the oppression and thus maintaining the status quo.

We have seen how those disorders judged to be the most severe are those which are most likely to be treated with physical interventions rather than with therapy or counselling. There appear to be further distinctions made by virtue of a person's class, race, gender, sexual orientation and other characteristics which might mark an individual as outside the majority group. People from oppressed groups are more likely to receive forcible treatment, and more likely to receive treatment with drugs and ECT. This includes women, people from black and minority ethnic groups, lesbian women and gay men, and older people. Service user groups have found that the majority of mental health service users would prefer to have access to the 'talking treatments' – counselling and psychotherapy. Access to such services is significantly affected by race, ethnicity and social class. Those least likely to be referred for counselling or therapy are older people, ethnic minorities, people with learning disabilities and those with serious mental health problems. The outlook is bleak for those who fall into more than one of these categories.

Gender

Women are more likely than men to be labelled mad. The mass of empirical data reveals women's dominance in the psychiatric statistics. There are variations within this; for example, women are far more likely to be diagnosed with depression or affective psychosis, whereas for schizophrenia the gender split is more or less equal (Cochrane, 1983; Ussher, 1991). Men are more likely to be compulsorily admitted for psychiatric treatment but women use psychiatric services more often and are prescribed twice as many psychotropic drugs as men (Prior, 1999). Women are also subjected to ECT treatment more often than men and, historically, were more likely to receive psychosurgery such as lobotomies (Ussher, 1991).

However, Prior draws attention to a changing trend; in 1991 men outnumbered women in psychiatric beds in Britain for the first time this century, the result of a process that began in the 1950s. As overall psychiatric bed numbers have decreased, the fall in the number of female patients has been more rapid than that in males. Prior explains this by a change in the conceptualization of mental disorder which gives more prominence to an individual's potential for dangerous behaviour – the perceived risk to the public. As men are more likely to be diagnosed with disorders which are associated with violent or disruptive behaviour – personality disorders, alcohol or drug-related disorders – they are more likely to be hospitalized (Prior, 1999). It could be, of course, that the stereotype of men as aggressive informs the perception of the nature of the disorders to which they seem to be more susceptible, rather than the other way round. The fact that involuntary psychiatric admissions are most likely to be young, black males would seem to support this notion. The association of aggression with the stereotype of blackness as well as maleness has a long history. The picture that emerges is one where legal powers are being used not just to ensure that people receive treatment, but rather to protect the public from a perceived risk – a perception, moreover, which is ill-founded. The stereotypes which still prevail are that women are mad, and men are mad, bad and dangerous. Thus women receive psychotropic medication and men are locked up, as evidenced by the fact that the psychiatric sections of the British prison system are occupied predominantly by men.

The fact remains, however, that when considering the overall use of psychiatric services, women heavily outnumber men. Feminist explanations for this fall into two categories: social causation and social construction. Social causation theories argue that the very nature of the traditional female role sends women mad. Gender inequality is endemic within society and within family life. Like other social institutions the family persists in forms that serve the interests of men, and often at women's expense; marriage is comparatively more beneficial to the psychological well-being of men than women (Cochrane, 1983; Williams, 1999). The traditional gender role definitions of male dominance and female submissiveness create a female susceptibility to psychological problems. Women's experience is thus of a lack of control over their own lives, which is a recognized factor in depression and other psychological disturbances.

The social construction view of women and mental health holds that psychiatric diagnoses are constructed by men on women. A patriarchal society is unable to tolerate female behaviour which challenges the norms of gender-defined roles; such behaviour, therefore, is labelled mad. This has the effect of locating the problem within the individual, and distracts attention from the social reality of that

person's life. Arguments for social constructionism are
supported by evidence that the stereotype of mental illness
is analogous with the stereotype of femaleness, concepts
related to maleness being closer to those associated with
the general norm of psychological health (Cochrane, 1983:
49). Despite Freud's ideas about the constitutionally bisexual nature of human beings, with the construction of both
masculinity and femininity being seen as precarious, post-
Freudian theorizing has identified mental health with gender orthodoxy, especially conventional heterosexuality and
marriage. Such formulations feed into the bias which
defines femininity itself as pathological. Jane Ussher cites a
study which ·demonstrated that, paradoxically, 'women
who *conform* to the female role model, as well as those who
reject it, are likely to be labelled psychiatrically ill' (Ussher,
1991: 168). In this study the stereotype of masculinity was
seen as the epitome of mental health – but only for men.
Women who are competitive, ambitious, independent, or
who reject the role of wife and mother, may be at risk of
being diagnosed as mentally ill. An example of how gender
stereotyping affects social and clinical assessments of
behaviour is in the expression of anger. Where anger might
be seen as an appropriate and normal aspect of behaviour
for a man, for women it can be seen as pathological.
Consequently, if a man expresses anger inappropriately, for
example through physical violence, he would be punished
by the legal system. A woman doing the same thing is more
likely to be sectioned.

Theories of social construction and causation are based
on a view of the respective positions of men and women
which are undoubtedly changing – there are social developments since the period of second-wave feminism which have
improved the position of many women in the western
world. But this is not true for all – social class plays a big
factor in this respect, the ameliorations in opportunity, education and status being most felt by the wealthier sectors of

society. Paradoxically there is now a growing group of such women who appear to be experiencing greater stress as a result of attempting to fulfil the roles of mother and home-maker as well as that of career woman. There are also many women who have not escaped from the 'traditional' female role – or who, indeed, choose to embrace that role. Given that gender inequality continues to exist throughout society, and that psychiatric diagnosis has an inherent gender bias, the feminist arguments continue to have validity today.

The implications of gender stereotyping can also have an impact on men's mental health. The stereotype of the strong bread-winning male is still very evident in western cultures. Being part of the dominant group (white, male, heterosexual, etc.) makes it hard to challenge the values and expectations of that group – you are unlikely to receive support from other members of the in-group by doing so. As Williams writes, 'even if men think that masculinity and the social and economic dominance of men might be a problem, they receive very little encouragement from each other to explore the implications' (Williams, 1999: 37). The male role is associated with success, strength, and the ability to support both themselves and a family; status and self-esteem are intimately connected with employment and achievement. Failure to meet those expectations can have severe consequences. Men who are unemployed, or retired, are at far greater risk of depression and other psychological problems than are women in the same situation. Men are also less likely to seek help – another consequence of the gender stereotype that men are strong and should be able to cope on their own.

There is much debate about the diagnosis of 'antisocial personality disorder', a label which men are far more likely to acquire than women. This is defined as 'the violation of the rights of others and a general lack of conformity to social norms' (Robins and Regier, 1991). Many mental health professionals regard this 'condition' as untreatable and it is often omitted from mental health statistics. Treating such behaviour as 'badness' leads to judicial enforcement and imprisonment; such a response is a symptom of a patriarchal society's intolerance of both male weakness and social deviance. Treating such behaviour as 'madness', however, is an inappropriate medicalization of something which has more to do with the wider social context than an individual's pathology. Both responses fail to take into account the implications of social deprivation and the impact of gender stereotyping.

Race and culture

The presence of racism in western cultures clearly has an effect on the mental health of the individuals within ethnic minorities (see Chapter 2). Being part of a socially marginalized group and being subject to prejudice and discrimination impacts on the psychological welfare of such people as well as on their opportunities for education, housing, employment and justice. All these factors lead to poor self-esteem, little social and political power, and low socioeconomic status. Internalized racism adds another element to the process of dehumanization.

Western psychiatry and psychotherapy are products of western culture. The history of psychological thought and theory includes notions such as the innate inferiority of black people, the benefits of slavery to the maintenance of the mental health of black Americans, and suchlike. While these ideas are patently discounted today, racism continues to permeate current psychiatric thought and practice. In both the US and Britain black people receive disproportionately high rates of diagnosis for the more severe mental disorders, in particular schizophrenia. Furthermore, blacks are over-represented among those patients who are compulsorily detained and are more likely to be given physical treatments rather than referred for psychotherapy (Fernando, 2002: 121). Mental health studies conducted in the general population on both sides of the Atlantic have found a lower prevalence of mental health disorders in black groups than in other ethnic groups, and yet the statistics on psychiatric diagnosis and admissions show completely the opposite picture (Prior, 1999: 38). The implication is inescapable that this has something to do with the relationship between the predominantly white medical profession and their black patients. As with the male stereotype, black people (particularly black men) are seen as violent. Black men are also viewed as unpredictable, lacking in insight and difficult to relate to – all good reasons for compulsory detention and psychotropic medication, and counter-indications for engaging with such a person in therapy or counselling.

A further element in the relationship between race, culture and mental disorders is the different ways in which people both express distress and interpret distress in others. The dominant western culture has specific notions about how we manifest psychological and physical pain; the application of these notions to those whose values and ideas are culturally different can lead to gross misunderstandings. Where the relationship between doctor and patient is informed by racist ideology and stereotypical notions engendering fear, the likelihood of a diagnosis of mental illness is increased. Similarly, culturally specific explanations and formulations of mental disorders can have an impact on both treatment and outcome. In countries where schizophrenia is viewed as a disorder which, after treatment, is cured, the outcome is far better than in those countries, like Britain, where the diagnosis of schizophrenia implies a lifelong disability with periods of remission (Cochrane, 1983; Warner, 1994). Although there are difficulties in standardizing the interpretation of symptoms and diagnosis in cross-cultural studies of schizophrenia, it appears to be the case that the outlook for people diagnosed with this condition in the third world is considerably better than for those in western cultures. Where the prevailing cultural belief is that people do recover from schizophrenia then that tends to happen, but where the prevailing belief is that it is an incurable disease then people tend to enter into a long-term career of illness. The fact that those so diagnosed in the west who reject the chronicity of their condition and their 'mental patient' status have a better prognosis would provide further evidence for this. In many African countries symptoms typically associated with schizophrenia are seen as temporary afflictions caused by external forces (supernatural or unknown). The individual is not an outcast, does not deserve blame or punishment and needs to be maintained in the community until the symptoms pass. In western societies we are both less optimistic regarding outcome and less tolerant of psychotic symptoms. Despite the benevolent-sounding policy of 'Care in the Community', this is precisely what we do not offer. Current or former psychiatric patients are isolated and excluded by western cultures. And because of the effects of racism and our unwillingness to attempt to understand the different ways in which ethnic groups other than our own may express and conceptualize psychological and mental distress, such groups are heavily over-represented in the population of psychiatric patients.

The process of 'culturizing racism' within psychiatry is described by Fernando as a trap that many fall into because of our reluctance to face up to our own racism. This is a process whereby injustices and disadvantages suffered by black and ethnic minorities are attributed to their own culture which causes them to behave in ways that are perceived as unhelpful or self-defeating. Examples of this would be by distorting patterns of illness (somatizing psychological symptoms), being too 'demanding' or too 'passive' (exaggerating symptoms or not expressing them), or not benefiting from treatment (communicating in ways that psychiatry sees as 'primitive'). In this way, Fernando tells us, 'the power of white over black is maintained because the explanations for "ethnic problems" are looked for in the "alien cultures" and the blame for the problems is attached to *them* – the "cultural aliens"' (Fernando, 2002: 123).

Sexuality

As I discussed in Chapter 4, notions about the 'pathology' or 'abnormality' of homosexuality and lesbianism go back a long way but received specific impetus with the growth of psychological theory at the beginning of the twentieth century. Modern society continues to find same-sex relationships problematic, and despite the declassification of homosexuality as a psychiatric disorder in 1973, the experiences of many gay men and lesbian women is that the medical profession, like the wider society, is unaccepting of life-styles that are outside stereotypical notions of 'normal' male and female behaviour.

Although homosexuality *per se* was declassified, it was replaced in the psychiatric classification systems first by 'sexual orientation disturbance' then by 'egodystonic homosexuality' and most recently by 'gender identity disorder'. Historically, homosexuals have been subjected to a plethora of treatments in misguided attempts to change their sexual orientation: ECT, brain surgery, castration and hormone injections. The current situation is that any attempt to change a person's sexual orientation is deemed unethical in the USA and highly questionable in Europe. Theoretically, therefore, only if a person has problems with his or her sexual orientation or identity should it come to psychiatric attention. The problem remains, however, in the assumption that any such difficulties are due to individual pathology rather than social intolerance. If 'gender identity disorder' is an official mental illness, then, in psychiatric terms, it is seen as residing within that individual's mind, brain, genes or biochemistry.

Like other minority groups, gay men and lesbian women are exposed to the stresses associated with social ostracism and prejudice. Being brought up in a society which has a predominantly negative view of sexual orientations other than heterosexuality can lead to internalized homophobia and a negative self-image. Unlike the factor of race, a person's sexual orientation is not immediately visible and apparent to others. The process of 'coming out' is in itself potentially stressful and requires a major shift in personal identity. Many gay men and lesbian women choose to 'pass' as straight in certain situations to avoid discrimination, particularly in the workplace, which creates a confusing and difficult double life. Whereas gay men and lesbian women do not wish to have their sexual orientation medicalized, there is a growing demand for their difficulties to be acknowledged. There are significantly higher rates of depression, substance abuse and attempted suicide among lesbians and gay men than among heterosexuals in both the USA and the UK (Davies and Neal, 1996; Herek, 1998). If we discount the possibility of inherent psychopathology within the homosexual population, then this is likely to be due to the heterosexism and homophobia in society at large, and the effects it has on those outside the heterosexual norm.

As sociological and socio-cultural theories about mental illness demonstrate, the incidence of psychological distress is closely associated with such factors as low socio-economic status, poverty, lack of support, poor educational and occupational opportunities or absence of material and financial independence. All research shows a consistent inverse relationship between wealth and mental disorders. The experience of being in a minority group, whatever that may be, is likely to increase the probability of an individual's being exposed to any or all of these sociological factors. Should they then become in any way mentally disturbed and, in addition, receive a psychiatric diagnosis, they will have achieved the dubious honour of having acquired double minority status.

What appears to be lacking in mainstream mental health services is a recognition of the significance of wider social factors on the mental health problems of those they treat. As with the lunacy policies of the nineteenth century, the mental health policies of the twentieth and twenty-first centuries have consistently reinforced the hierarchical divisions between rich and poor, men and women, heterosexuals and homosexuals and between majority and minority racial groups.

6 | Conclusion

IT IS IRREFUTABLE THAT THE situation for all minority groups, socially, politically and economically, has improved significantly over the last fifty years. All too often, however, such improvements are seen as obviating the necessity for further social action. Relative progress is mistaken for an indication that inequalities and injustices in the form of discriminatory attitudes and practices no longer exist or need to be addressed. Despite the manifest amelioration in the situation of people for whom an element of their being or experience puts them outside the social mainstream, there is still an unacceptable level of prejudice and discrimination meted out to such people in all areas of their lived experience. To ignore that, or to pretend that it does not exist, simply adds to the injustice.

One of the things that emerges from my examination of various aspects of an individual's identity which have the potential to attract prejudice and adverse discrimination is the problematic way in which we use language within this context. Despite the fact that in many instances there is considerable doubt about the validity or relevance of strict distinctions between groups that are perceived as different in some respects, the language we use to describe such differences has the effect of fostering the impression of huge unbridgeable gulfs between the people in whom they are located. Thus we talk about 'black' and 'white' people when we know that many, if not all, of us are of mixed descent, our ancestors possibly originating in many different cultural and racial traditions. Similarly, we use the terms 'heterosexual' and 'homosexual' as though they indicated two definitively separate groups. In fact people's sexual experiences, inclinations, practices and fantasies span a far wider spectrum than these terms alone imply. 'Sanity' and 'insanity' too are set up as dichotomous states, with little cognizance given to the vast area between them, a place which many of us inhabit much of the time. Likewise gender is perceived as a polarity, with considerably more emphasis being laid on the differences and distinctions between men and women than on their similarities, or on the fact that we are all a blend of the stereotypical 'male' qualities and attributes and the stereotypical 'female' ones, regardless of our actual gender.

My belief is that we use language in this way precisely because of the need to categorize, fix, encapsulate those elements of being which we find disturbing or threatening. By creating firm divisions between groups in this way there is the implication that the boundaries are impermeable and the 'otherness' is 'out there'. Identity is fundamentally relational – at base it boils down to 'me' and 'not me'. If I am white, then I cannot be black. If I am sane, I cannot be insane. If I am heterosexual, I cannot be homosexual. If I am female, I cannot be male. In this way we attempt to fix and affirm our sense of identity and blind ourselves to the complexities of being of which we are all composed. Being confronted with another person who embodies 'otherness' is therefore alarming and has the potential to undermine our shaky sense of confidence in who we think we are.

One response to this discomfort with difference is the attempt to make the 'other' more like us. This can be seen in calls for immigrants to 'assimilate' and 'integrate' – to give up their cultural practices and religious beliefs and adopt the customs and life-style of the majority group. It is also evidenced in the view that sees homosexuality as an aberration, something to be overcome or 'cured', thus returning the individual to the 'normal' state of hetero-sexuality. Interestingly, it is also evident in certain elements of feminist doctrine, where emphasis is laid on succeeding in a man's world by being as much like men as possible, and denying or denigrating 'feminine' attributes.

Another, more covert, response is to adopt an attitude whereby we deliberately, or unconsciously, ignore differences. In an interpersonal encounter we may choose not to register another person's skin colour, or to disregard their homosexuality. On one level this can be seen as laudable – we are acknowledging our shared humanity rather than focusing on those elements which could be perceived as marking us out as different from one another. However, this response also has the effect of ignoring or denying an important part of the other person's identity. This is a response which I suspect occurs frequently within therapy and is often clothed in respectability by calling it 'being non-judgemental' – a stance which most therapeutic models would hold up as a goal for the practitioner to strive for, but which can be misunderstood as meaning ignoring those elements of another person's being which provoke judge-ment. I suspect that what underlies this type of response is the desire to relate exclusively with those aspects of the other with which we can resonate or identify – partly because that has the effect of reinforcing our own identity, and partly because those elements we are ignoring are the ones that have the potential to make us feel uncomfortable, anxious or threatened. In effect, this response is the direct opposite of that which sees a person as characterized *only* by their element of difference – their race, or gender, or sexual orientation – and takes that to be the sum total of their identity. Either extreme fails to take account of the person in their totality, and as such diminishes them and restricts the possibility of our relating with them on all levels of their being.

When any of these responses take place in a social encounter they can be experienced as exclusionary, patronizing or downright discriminatory, depending on the extent to which they are conveyed or perceived. When they take place within counselling or psychotherapy the implications are, in my view, far worse. At the very least they would seriously undermine the potential for any effective therapy to occur. At worst they could be experienced as demeaning or abusive.

The language we use, therefore, has the effect of categorizing and pigeon-holing people into groups. Groups are assigned worth and importance to varying degrees depending on a variety of factors, not the least of which is the judgement of what is 'normal', 'acceptable' or 'natural'. Such words appear, at first glance, to convey some objective standard. In fact what they usually mean is the behaviour, beliefs, attitudes and values of the majority group. Within all societies there exist established social categories, the maintenance of which is in the interests of the largest group of people. For this reason society is always prejudiced towards the protection of established categories and resistant to their being threatened. That such an arrangement is to the detriment of any minority group is self-evident – in a sense social inequalities structure society, and are also deeply embedded in our personal identities.

The need to be aware of these issues is particularly pertinent for anyone within the field of counselling and psychotherapy precisely because these are enterprises which lay claim to providing a service which enables people to address the full scope of their personal issues and examine all aspects of their being; they also purport to do so within the context of an objective, accepting and non-judgemental professional relationship. If, as I have suggested, these activities are themselves blinkered by unacknowledged prejudices and limitations, and are informed by theories and attitudes which are in fact reflective of only one sector of society, that is to say the majority or mainstream, then those of us involved in these professions have a duty, at the very least, to acknowledge these limitations, or, preferably, to attempt to address them.

One of the things that emerges clearly from my research into the treatment of difference within counselling and psychotherapy is the extent to which the theories on which these activities are founded are themselves infused with concepts which perpetuate the normative values of the majority social group – that is to say white, western, middle-class and heterosexual. Although many of the early theories also carry a sexist (that is, male-oriented) bias, within contemporary practice the emphasis is decidedly in favour of 'female' qualities and modes of expression, to the detriment or even denigration of 'male' attributes. The danger lies in the fact that not only are these biases largely unrecognized, but the theories and practices enshrined within psychotherapy and counselling, and passed on within their training courses, are presented as a kind of universal psychological template or blueprint, applicable to all people regardless of their individual circumstances in terms of social position, race, culture or life-style choices. The fact that psychotherapy and counselling training courses fail to attract (or fail to accept?) students from all minority groups (and in this context I would define men as a minority group), and that such groups are also significantly underrepresented as clients of counselling and psychotherapy would seem to confirm that such biases are indeed in operation and that there is a lamentable failure on the part of psychotherapy and counselling to meet the needs of the individuals in these groups.

As I discussed in the first chapter, the process of discriminating, making comparisons and choices and distinguishing our preferences is something we all engage in all the time. It involves an awareness of similarities and differences; it also involves judgements based on these distinctions as well as on our individual tastes, views and moral values. The vital factor is to be aware of the judgements and choices we are making and also to be aware of the criteria on which those judgements are based.

As counsellors and psychotherapists it is essential to be aware in several distinct and interlocking areas. Firstly, we need to be aware of the social influences that have inevitably impacted upon us. By virtue of growing up in a society which is infused with notions which are prejudiced against certain groups perceived as different, our environmental heritage inevitably contains elements of sexism, hetero-sexism and homophobia, racism and other discriminatory attitudes towards minority groups. We need to be aware of our own internal prejudices and accept that, like many aspects of who we are, it may not be possible to completely eradicate them. However, being aware of the capacity they have to affect our responses to others allows us to make choices which override them.

Secondly, we need to inform ourselves of the experiences of those people who are outside the social mainstream. We need to find out about their life-styles, and the difficulties they encounter by virtue of being in some way different from the majority – difficulties which, if we are part of that majority ourselves, we have never personally encountered. Thirdly, we need to be aware of the limitations endemic within the theories and practice of psychotherapy and counselling. Only if we are aware of the normative bias within the tenets of many psychotherapeutic models will we be able to challenge and transcend such a bias. Fourthly, we need to be aware of the various dimensions of difference that can exist between practitioner and client: gender, race, culture, class, age, sexual orientation, mental and physical capacity. We need to be sensitive to how such differences impact on the therapeutic relationship and be willing to address these issues with our clients appropri-ately, owning the elements we ourselves bring to the encounter and in full cognizance of the attitude of society at large.

Finally, I would urge all practitioners of psychotherapy and counselling and all students training to become practitioners to adopt a questioning and critical stance to the theories and ethos of their training and the institutions and facilities in which they work. Individually we need to confront and challenge the normative and prejudiced influences to which we are subjected in order to ensure that we do not bring those either to our work or to our social encounters. The goal has to be that of recognizing the value of difference, eschewing the assumption that different means worse, or less than, or incomplete or abnormal. On the contrary, we need to acknowledge that differences add richness, complexity and variety and as such should be embraced.

Bibliography

Alibhai-Brown, Y. (2001) *Mixed Feelings*. London: The Women's Press Ltd.

Archer, J. and Lloyd, B. (1985) *Sex and Gender*. Cambridge: Cambridge University Press.

Aries, P. and Bejin, A. (1982) *Western Sexuality*. Oxford: Blackwell.

BAC (1998) *Code of Ethics and Practice for Counsellors*. Rugby: British Association for Counselling.

BACP (2002) *Ethical Framework for Good Practice in Counselling and Psychotherapy*. Rugby: British Association for Counselling and Psychotherapy.

Banton, M. (1994) *Discrimination*. Buckingham: Open University Press.

Banton, M. (1997) *Ethnic and Racial Consciousness*. Harlow: Longman.

Barham, P. (1992) *Closing the Asylum*. Harmondsworth: Penguin.

Bass, E. and Davis, L. (1988) *The Courage to Heal*. New York: Harper Perennial.

Bateson, G., Jackson, D., Haley, J. and Weakland, J. (1956) 'Toward a theory of schizophrenia', *Behavioral Science*, 1: 251–64.

Becker, H. (1963) *Outsiders*. New York: Free Press.

Bennett, D. and Morris, I. (1983) 'Deinstitutionalization in the United Kingdom', *International Journal of Mental Health*, 11 (4): 5–23.

Biddiss, M. (1966) 'Gobineau and the origins of European racism', *Race*, 7 (3).

Bleuler, M. (1972) *The Schizophrenic Disorders: Long-Term Patient and Family Studies*. New Haven: Yale University Press.

Bowers, L. (1998) *The Social Nature of Mental Illness*. London: Routledge.

Breggin, P. (1993) *Toxic Psychiatry*. London: Fontana.

Bulmer, M. and Solomos, J. (eds) (1999) *Racism*. Oxford: Oxford University Press.

Carter, R.T. (1995) *The Influence of Race and Racial Identity in Psychotherapy*. New York: Wiley.

Chaplin, J. (1988) *Feminist Counselling in Action*. London: Sage.

Chaplin, J. (1989) 'Counselling and gender', in W. Dryden, D. Charles-Edwards and R. Woolfe (eds), *Handbook of Counselling in Britain*. London: Routledge.

Chesler, P. (1972) *Women and Madness*. New York: Doubleday.

Chodorow, N.J. (1994) *Femininities, Masculinities, Sexualities*. London: Free Association Books.

Clare, A. (2001) *On Men – Masculinity in Crisis*. London: Arrow.

Cochrane, R. (1983) *The Social Creation of Mental Illness*. Harlow: Longman.

Coldridge, L. and Mickelborough, P. (2003) 'Who's counting? Access to UK counsellor training: a demographic profile of trainees on four courses', *Counselling and Psychotherapy Research*, 3 (1): 72–5.

Cornforth, S. (2001) 'Culture: the song without words', *Counselling and Psychotherapy Research*, 1 (3): 194–9.

Cowen, P.J. and Wood, A.J. (1991) 'Editorial: biological markers of depression', *Psychological Medicine*, 21: 831–6.

Crawford, P. (ed.) (1983) *Exploring Women's Past*. Hemel Hempstead: George Allen & Unwin.

CRE (Commission for Racial Equality) (1999a) *Housing and Homelessness*. London: CRE.

CRE (Commission for Racial Equality) (1999b) *Ethnic Minorities in Britain*. London: CRE.

Cross, M.C. and Papadopoulos, L. (2001) *Becoming a Therapist*. Hove: Brunner-Routledge.

Curtin, P. (1965) *The Image of Africa: British Ideas and Action 1780–1850*. London: Macmillan.

d'Ardenne, P. and Mahtani, A. (1989) *Transcultural Counselling in Action*. London: Sage.

Davies, D. and Neal, C. (1996) *Pink Therapy*. Buckingham: Open University Press.

Davies, D. and Neal, C. (eds) (2000a) *Therapeutic Perspectives on Working with Lesbian, Gay and Bisexual Clients*. Buckingham: Open University Press.

Davies, D. and Neal, C. (eds) (2000b) *Issues in Therapy with Lesbian, Gay, Bisexual and Transgendered Clients*. Buckingham: Open University Press.

Dawkins, R. (1976) *The Selfish Gene*. Oxford: Oxford University Press.

de Gobineau, A. (1999) *The Inequality of Human Races*. New York: Howard Fertig.

D'Emilio, J. (1991) 'Gay politics and community in San Francisco since world war two', in M.B. Duberman, M. Vicinus and G. Chauncy (eds), *Hidden From History*. Harmondsworth: Penguin.

DeVos, G., Marsella, A.J. and Hsu, F.L.K. (1985) 'Introduction: approaches to culture and self', in A.J. Marsella, G. DeVos and F.L.K. Hsu (eds), *Culture and Self: Asian and Western Perspectives*. New York and London: Tavistock Publications.

DiPlacido, J. (1998) 'Minority stress among lesbians, gay men, and bisexuals: a consequence of heterosexism, homophobia, and stigmatization', in G. Herek (ed.), *Psychological Perspectives on Lesbian and Gay Issues: Volume 4, Stigma and Sexual Orientation: Understanding Prejudice against Lesbians, Gay Men, and Bisexuals*. Thousands Oaks: Sage.

Dollimore, J. (1991) *Sexual Dissidence*. Oxford: Oxford University Press.

Duberman, M.B., Vicinus, M. and Chauncey, G. (eds) (1991) *Hidden from History*. Harmondsworth: Penguin.

EOC (Equal Opportunities Commission) (2001) *Facts About Women and Men in Great Britain 2001*. EOC website.

Evans, M. (1997) *Introducing Contemporary Feminist Thought*. Cambridge: Polity Press.

Fanon, F. (1986) *Black Skin, White Masks*. London: Pluto Press.

Fernando, S. (2002) *Mental Health, Race and Culture*. Basingstoke: Palgrave.

Fone, B. (2000) *Homophobia*. New York: Picador.

Foucault, M. (1965) *Madness and Civilization: A History of Insanity in the Age of Reason*. New York: Random House.

Foucault, M. (1976) *The History of Sexuality*. Harmondsworth: Penguin.

Franklin, K. (1998) 'Unassuming motivations: contextualizing the narratives of antigay assailants', in G. Herek (ed.), *Psychological Perspectives on Lesbian and Gay Issues: Volume 4, Stigma and Sexual Orientation: Understanding Prejudice against Lesbians, Gay Men, and Bisexuals*. Thousands Oaks: Sage.

Fredrickson, G. (1988) *The Arrogance of Race: Historical Perspectives on Slavery, Racism and Social Inequality*. Middletown: Wesleyan University Press.

Fredrickson, G.M. (2002) *Racism: A Short History*. Princeton: Princeton University Press.

Freedman, J. (2001) *Feminism*. Buckingham: Open University Press.

Freud, S. (1905) *Three Essays on the Theory of Sexuality*. Penguin Freud Library 7. Harmondsworth: Penguin.

Freud, S. (1916–17) *Introductory Lectures on Psychoanalysis*. Penguin Freud Library 1. Harmondsworth: Penguin.

Freud, S. (1920) *The Psychogenesis of a Case of Homosexuality in a Woman*. Penguin Freud Library 9. Harmondsworth: Penguin.

Freud, S. (1933) *Femininity*. Standard Edition 22: 112–25. London: Hogarth.

Friedan, B. (1992) *The Feminine Mystique*. Harmondsworth: Penguin.

Fromm-Reichmann, F. (1943) 'Psychoanalytic psychotherapy with psychotics: the influence of modifications in technique on present trends in psychoanalysis', in D. Bullard (ed.) (1959) *Frieda Fromm-Reichmann: Psychoanalysis and Psychotherapy*. Chicago: University of Chicago Press.

Fromm-Reichmann, F. (1952) 'Some aspects of psychoanalytic psychotherapy with schizophrenics', in M. Brody and F. Redlich (eds), *Psychotherapy with Schizophrenics*. New York: International University Press.

Galton, F. (1998) *Hereditary Genius*. Chicago: University of Chicago Press.

Garde, J. (2003) 'Masculinity and madness', *Counselling and Psychotherapy Research*, 3 (1): 6–15.

Gillon, E. (2002) 'Counselling training and social exclusion', *Counselling and Psychotherapy Journal*, 13 (3): 24–7.

Gilman, S.L. (1985) *Difference and Pathology*. Ithaca: Cornell University Press.

Goffman, E. (1961) *Asylums*. Harmondsworth: Penguin.

Goffman, E. (1963) *Stigma*. London: Penguin.

Gottesman, I.I. (1991) *Schizophrenia Genesis: The Origins of Madness*. New York: W.H. Freeman.

Goulbourne, H. (1998) *Race Relations in Britain since 1945*. Basingstoke: Macmillan.

Griffith, V. (2002) 'Wires crossed over genes', *Financial Times*, 2 November.

Haley, J. (1967) 'Toward a theory of pathological systems', in P. Watzlawick and J. Weakland (eds), *The Interactional View*. New York: W.W. Norton.

Halperin, D. (1998) 'Saint Foucault', in N. Zack, L. Shrage and C. Sartwell (eds), *Race, Class, Gender and Sexuality: The Big Questions*. Oxford: Blackwell.

Hamer, D. (1994) *The Science of Desire: The Search for the Gay Gene and the Biology of Behaviour*. New York: Simon & Schuster.

Harding, C. (ed.) (2001) *Sexuality*. Hove: Brunner-Routledge.

Harris, V. (1998) 'Prison of color', in N. Zack, L. Shrage and C. Sartwell (eds), *Race, Class, Gender and Sexuality: The Big Questions*. Oxford: Blackwell.

Haussen, A. (1991) 'Sodomy in the Dutch Republic during the eighteenth century', in M.B. Duberman, M. Vicinus and G. Chauncy (eds), *Hidden From History*. Harmondsworth: Penguin.

Herek, G. (ed.) (1998) *Psychological Perspectives on Lesbian and Gay issues: Volume 4, Stigma and Sexual Orientation: Understanding Prejudice against Lesbians, Gay Men, and Bisexuals*. Thousand Oaks: Sage.

Herrnstein, R.J. and Murray, C. (1994) *The Bell Curve*. New York: Free Press.

Hillman, J. and Ventura, M. (1992) *We've Had a Hundred Years of Psychotherapy – and the World's Getting Worse*. New York: HarperCollins.

Holmes, C. (1991) *A Tolerant Country*. London: Faber & Faber.

Horney, K. (1924) 'On the genesis of the castration complex in women', *International Journal of Psychoanalysis*, 32: 644–57.

Horney, K. (1973) *Feminine Psychology*. New York: W.W. Norton.

Howells, J.G. (1991) 'Schizophrenia in the medieval period', in J.G. Howells (ed.), *The Concept of Schizophrenia*. Washington: American Psychiatric Press, pp. 29–46.

Izzard, S. (2000) 'Psychoanalytic psychotherapy', in D. Davies and C. Neal (eds), *Therapeutic Perspectives on Working with Lesbian, Gay and Bisexual Clients*. Buckingham: Open University Press.

Jeffery-Poulter, S. (1991) *Peers, Queers and Commons*. London: Routledge.

Jenner, F.A., Monteiro, A., Zagalo-Cardoson, J.A. and Cunha-Oliviera, J.A. (1993) *Schizophrenia: A Disease or Some Ways of Being Human?* Sheffield: Sheffield Academic Press.

Jones, E.E. (1982) 'Psychotherapists' impressions of treatment outcome as a function of race', *Journal of Clinical Psychology*, 38: 722–31.

Jung, C. (1991) *The Psychogenesis of Mental Disease*. London: Routledge.

Kareem, J. and Littlewood, R. (eds) (2000) *Intercultural Therapy*. Oxford: Blackwell Science.

Karon, B. (1992) 'The fear of understanding schizophrenia', *Psychoanalytic Psychology*, 9 (2): 191–211.

Karon, B. and VandenBos, G. (1981) *Psychotherapy of Schizophrenia*. Northvale: Aronson.

Katz, J.H. (1985) 'The sociopolitical nature of counselling', *The Counseling Psychologist*, 13 (4): 615–24.

Kinsey, A., Pomeroy, W. and Martin, C. (1948) *Sexual Behavior in the Human Male*. Philadelphia, PA: W.B. Saunders.

Kinsey, A., Pomeroy, W. and Martin, C. (1953) *Sexual Behavior in the Human Female*. Philadelphia: W.B. Saunders.

Krafft-Ebing, R. von (1931) *Psychopathia Sexualis*. Brooklyn: Physicians and Surgeons Book Co.

Laing, R.D. (1960) *The Divided Self*. Harmondsworth: Penguin.

Laing, R.D. (1967) *The Politics of Experience*. Harmondsworth: Penguin.

Laplanche, J. and Pontalis, J.B. (1973) *The Language of Psychoanalysis*. London: Karnac.

Lawrence, M. and Maguire, M. (1997) *Psychotherapy with Women*. Basingstoke: Macmillan.

Lemma-Wright, A. (1995) *Invitation to Psychodynamic Psychology*. London: Whurr.

Lerner, G. (1986) *The Creation of Patriarchy*. Oxford: Oxford University Press.

Lidz, T. (1975) *The Origin and Treatment of Schizophrenic Disorders*. Madison: International Universities Press.

Litman, G.K. (1978) 'Clinical aspects of sex-role stereotyping', in J. Chetwynd and O. Hartnett (eds), *The Sex-Role System*. London: Routledge & Kegan Paul.

Littlewood, R. and Lipsedge, M. (1989) *Aliens and Alienists*. London: Unwin Hyman.

McLeod, E. (1994) *Women's Experience of Feminist Therapy and Counselling*. Buckingham: Open University Press.

MacMaster, N. (2001) *Racism in Europe*. Basingstoke: Palgrave.

Mair, D. (2003) 'Gay men's experiences of counselling', *Counselling and Psychotherapy Research*, 3 (1): 33–41.

Miles, R. (1993) *The Women's History of the World*. London: HarperCollins.

Millar, A. (2003) 'Men's experience of considering counselling: entering the unknown', *Counselling and Psychotherapy Research*, 3 (1): 16–24.

Mind Policy Briefing (2002a) '10 questions about compulsory treatment in the community', *www.mind.org.uk*.

Mind Policy Briefing (2002b) 'Creating accepting communities', *www.mind.org.uk*.

Moir, A. and Jessel, D. (1989) *Brain Sex*. London: Mandarin.

Money, J. (1988) *Gay, Straight, and In-Between*. Oxford: Oxford University Press.

Moorhouse, S. (2000) 'Quantitative research in intercultural therapy: some methodological considerations', in J. Kareem and R. Littlewood (eds), *Intercultural Therapy*. Oxford: Blackwell Science.

Mort, F. (1987) *Dangerous Sexualities*. London: Routledge & Kegan Paul.

Mosher, L.R. and Menn, A.Z. (1978) 'Community residential treatment for schizophrenia: two-year follow-up', *Hospital and Community Psychiatry*, 29: 715–23.

Mosse, G. (1985) *Toward the Final Solution*. New York: Howard Fertig.

Newnes, C. (1999) 'Histories of psychiatry', in C. Newnes, G. Holmes and C. Dunn (eds), *This is Madness*. Ross-on-Wye: PCCS Books.

Nicholson, L. (1998) 'Interpreting gender', in N. Zack, L. Shrage and C. Sartwell (eds), *Race, Class, Gender and Sexuality: The Big Questions*. Oxford: Blackwell.

Orbach, S. and Eichenbaum, L. (1984) *What Do Women Want?* London: Fontana.

Orbach, S. and Eichenbaum, L. (1985) *Understanding Women*. Harmondsworth: Penguin.

Palmer, S. and Laungani, P. (1999), *Counselling in a Multicultural Society*. London: Sage.

Perry, J. (1972) 'Psychosis as visionary state', *Journal of Analytic Psychology*, 17 (2): 184–98.

Pilgrim, D. (1990) 'Competing histories of madness', in R. Bentall (ed.), *Reconstructing Schizophrenia*. London: Routledge.

Pinker, S. (2002) *The Blank Slate*. London: Allen Lane.

Porter, R. (1987) *A Social History of Madness*. London: Weidenfeld & Nicolson.

Porter, R. (2002) *Madness: A Brief History*. Oxford: Oxford University Press.

Prior, P.M. (1999) *Gender and Mental Health*. Basingstoke: Macmillan.

Queen, C. and Schimel, L. (eds) (1997) *PoMoSexuals*. San Francisco: Cleiss Press.

Rack, P. (1982) *Race, Culture and Mental Disorder*. London: Tavistock.

Robins, L. and Regier, D. (eds) (1991) *Psychiatric Disorders in America: The Epidemiologic Catchment Area Study*. New York: Free Press.

Rose, C. (2002) 'Talking gender but who's listening?', *Counselling and Psychotherapy Journal*, 13 (7): 6–9.

Rose, S., Lewontin, R.C. and Kamin, L.J. (1984) *Not in Our Genes*. Harmondsworth: Penguin.

Rowan, J. (1987) *The Horned God*. London: Routledge & Kegan Paul.

Rowbotham, S. (1999) *A Century of Women*. Buckingham: Open University Press.

Satinover, J. (1998) *Homosexuality and the Politics of Truth*. Grand Rapids: Hamewith.

Scull, A. (1981) *Madhouses, Mad-Doctors and Madmen*. Pennsylvania: University of Pennsylvania Press.

Scull, A. (1984) *Decarceration*. Cambridge: Polity Press.

Sedgwick, P. (1982) *Psycho Politics*. London: Pluto Press.

Seligman, M.E.P. and Rosenhan, D.L. (1998) *Abnormality*. New York: W.W. Norton.

Serban, G. (1979) 'Mental status, functioning and stress in chronic schizophrenic patients in community care', *American Journal of Psychiatry*, 136: 948–52.

Simon, A. (1998) 'The relationship between stereotypes of and attitudes towards lesbians and gays', in G. Herek (ed.), *Psychological Perspectives on Lesbian and Gay Issues: Volume 4, Stigma and Sexual Orientation: Understanding Prejudice against Lesbians, Gay Men, and Bisexuals*. Thousands Oaks: Sage.

Sketchley, J. (1989) 'Counselling and sexual orientation', in W. Dryden, D. Charles-Edwards and R. Woolfe (eds), *Handbook of Counselling in Britain*. London: Routledge.

Smith, E.M.J. (1985) 'Ethnic minorities: life stress, social support and mental health issues', *The Counseling Psychologist*, 13 (4): 537–79.

Snowden, F.M. (1983) *Before Color Prejudice*. Cambridge, MA: Harvard University Press.

Spinelli, E. (2001) *The Mirror and the Hammer*. London: Continuum.

Stevens, A. and Price, J. (1996) *Evolutionary Psychiatry*. London: Routledge.

Stoller, R. (1968) *Sex and Gender*. New York: Science House.

Stoller, R. (1985) *Presentations of Gender*. New Haven: Yale University Press.

Stone, M.H. (1991) 'The psychodynamics of schizophrenia I' and 'The psychodynamics of schizophrenia II', in J.G. Howells (ed.), *The Concept of Schizophrenia*. Washington: American Psychiatric Press, pp. 125–72.

Sue, D.W., Arendondo, P. and McDivis, R.J. (1992) 'Multicultural counselling competencies and standards: a call to the profession', *Journal of Counselling and Development*, 70: 477–81.

Sullivan, H.S. (1924) *Schizophrenia as a Human Process*. New York: W.W. Norton.

Szasz, T. (1962) *The Myth of Mental Illness*. London: Paladin.

Szasz, T. (1970) *The Manufacture of Madness*. London: Routledge & Kegan Paul.

Szasz, T. (1976) *Schizophrenia: The Sacred Symbol of Psychiatry*. New York: Basic Books.

Szasz, T. (2002) *Liberation by Oppression*. New Brunswick: Transaction Publishers.

Triandis, H. (1985) 'Some major dimensions of cultural variation in client populations', in P. Pedersen (ed.), *Handbook of Cross-Cultural Counseling and Therapy*. Westport: Greenwood Press.

Trumbach, R. (1991) 'The birth of the queen: sodomy and the emergence of gender equality in modern culture, 1660–1750', in M.B. Duberman, M. Vicinus and G. Chauncy (eds), *Hidden From History*. Harmondsworth: Penguin.

Tuckwell, G. (2001) 'The threat of the other: using mixed quantitative and qualitative methods to elucidate racial and cultural dynamics in the counselling process', *Counselling and Psychotherapy Research*, 1 (3): 194–9.

Ussher, J. (1991) *Women's Madness*. New York: Harvester Wheatsheaf.

Verrier, N.N. (1993) *The Primal Wound*. Baltimore: Gateway Press Inc.

Warner, R. (1994) *Recovery from Schizophrenia*. London: Routledge.
Weeks, J. (1977) *Coming Out: Homosexual Politics in Britain from the Nineteenth Century to the Present*. London: Quartet.
Weeks, J. (1985) *Sexuality and its Discontents*. London: Routledge.
Weeks, J. (1991) *Against Nature*. London: Rivers Oram Press.
Wheeler, S. (2003) 'Men and therapy: are they compatible?', *Counselling and Psychotherapy Research*, 3 (1): 3–5.
Williams, J. (1999) 'Social inequalities and mental health', in C. Newnes, G. Holmes and C. Dunn (eds), *This is Madness*. Ross-on-Wye: PCCS Books.
Wilson, E.O. (1975) *Sociobiology: The New Synthesis*. Cambridge, MA: Harvard University Press.
Woodward, K. (ed.) (1997) *Identity and Difference*. London: Sage.
Young, V. (1995) *The Equality Complex*. New York: Cassell.
Zack, N., Shrage, L. and Sartwell, C. (eds) (1998) *Race, Class, Gender and Sexuality: The Big Questions*. Oxford: Blackwell.

Index